HOLIDAY COOKING ABROAD

Holiday Cooking Abroad

in France, Italy and Spain

By

JANE ROSS

assisted by

JEAN ROSS

CHATTO & WINDUS

Published by
Chatto & Windus Ltd
42 William IV Street
London W.C.2

*

Clarke, Irwin & Co. Ltd
Toronto

ISBN 0 7011 1621 8

First published 1971

© Jane Ross 1971

Printed in Great Britain by
Northumberland Press Limited
Gateshead

ACKNOWLEDGMENTS

We should like to thank all the people who have patiently answered so many questions, contributed recipes, read through the manuscript and checked up on local food for us. In particular we are most grateful to the Buré and Archambault families (Paris and Normandy), Esther Whitfield and Audrey Glynn (Villajoyosa, Spain), Norman Tapp (Ibiza), Margaret Santín (Jesolo, Italy) and Signor Migliorini (Villas Italia).

CONTENTS

Introduction

There are endless books on cooking continental food in one's own kitchen, but this book is for those of us who want to cook in a continental kitchen when on holiday. More and more people are taking their holidays in Europe, in a rented villa or flat, caravanning or camping. Too often one finds that the cook who is hired with the villa turns out to be unable to cook at all, or she only cooks things you don't like, or perhaps worst of all, she is so wildly extravagant that all your spending money evaporates in a couple of abandoned flips round the market. (This type has the distressing habit of buying in bulk and taking the unwanted remains home as 'perks'.)

More often, however, shopping and cooking fall to the holiday-maker. They can be the greatest fun but in unfamiliar surroundings can take twice as long and, combined with language difficulties and the mysteries of the metric system, can waste precious time. Labels on tins occasionally give the names of the contents in different languages but the translations can be mystifying and frequently vie with menus for inaccuracy—like the enticing description of *hors d'oeuvres* as 'varied outworks'.

Inadequate cooking facilities can also be a nightmare. We have suffered from kitchens in several countries, like the one in Spain, tiled in cyclamen pink, where not a drop of water came out of the taps, and the most modern gadget was a pestle and mortar; or the kitchen in France which, far from being a temple of gastronomy, contained one saucepan and a terrifying electric stove that gave one shocks. Of course, cooking habits and equipment vary from one country to another but it helps to be forewarned.

We have tried to give a general idea of what to find in the shops, markets and kitchens of France, Italy and Spain. Without giving actual prices, which fluctuate, we have indicated what is cheap and what is so expensive to buy that it's worth taking the equivalent out from home if you possibly can. Some food which we take for granted is unobtainable, so that trying to reproduce what we eat at home is either impossible or tastes so different that it's not worth doing. Baked beans on toast might seem the simplest snack in the world—but abroad the beans could cost three times as much, there may be no grill to make toast, and anyway the bread is the wrong shape. On the other hand, strange vegetables and sinister sausages which we might regard with deep suspicion at home often turn out delicious. We have tried to encourage experiment.

In the recipe section the lists of ingredients are given in English, French, Italian and Spanish, so they can be used as shopping lists to save ferreting through phrase books. The ingredients (or nearest equivalent) can be found in all three countries. We have given metric weights where you will need them for shopping, but for measuring amounts in the kitchen we have used cups, teaspoons and tablespoons. Some of the recipes can be partly prepared in advance, and nearly all of them can be cooked on top of the stove.

The safest way to avoid a disastrous time in your holiday kitchen is to find out as much as possible about it before you go so that you can take with you any vital equipment. We have found four things indispensable—a non-stick pan for easy washing-up, a pressure cooker to save time and fuel, an asbestos mat for simmering food on a gas ring, and a roll of aluminium foil.

We hope this book will add to the enjoyment of your holiday by giving you a carefree time in the kitchen and by introducing you to new flavours and dishes. You may even be tempted to try them out again at home and rediscover some favourite holiday food at your local delicatessen.

FRANCE

General

In France the cost of living is so high that it is not a question of not being able to obtain some groceries but of not being able to afford them. Meat and butter are prohibitive, hotly followed by soft drinks and tinned foods. Everyday wine is about the only thing costing less than in England, plus some liqueurs and apéritifs. Vegetables, fruit, milk, bread and pasta are reasonable, for France, but still a bit more than we would expect to pay here.

The one consolation is that the quality of food is high, the variety enormous and the shops clean. Prices do vary according to the district: Paris, the north and round the coastal resorts are all expensive areas; the cheapest are around the Massif Central and some of the southern provinces, well inland. If you are staying by the sea, it would pay you to go to the nearest market town inland. Some of the bigger towns have a permanent market, others hold a street market once or twice a week. You can find out from the local Syndicat d'Initiative.

It seems awful to suggest going to such a gastronomic country loaded up with food, but the best way to economise is to take as much butter as possible and, if you have room, something like a cooked turkey, ham or large joint to cook when you get there. Insulated cases keep the food fresh in transit for up to eight hours. Tinned meats are another way to eke out the budget, but it seems unadventurous when there are so many delicious things to buy at the Charcuterie (see p. 23) which, served with a salad or vegetables, make a cheapish meal. Taking soft drinks and cereals is another money-saver and means one can then afford the more exciting things you wouldn't get at home.

The shops' opening hours are from 8, 8.30 or 9 a.m. to 7, 7.30 or 8 p.m. Many do not shut for lunch, but further south they are closed for two or three hours. The food shops are all open on Sunday mornings till midday—some will even stay open in the afternoon in the season in tourist areas. However, many shops are shut all day on Monday, though in towns there is usually a bakery selling fresh bread. The national holidays, when banks and shops are firmly closed, are as follows:

New Year's Day
Easter Monday
1st May (Labour Day)
Ascension Day
Whit Monday
14th July (Bastille Day)
15th August (Assumption)
1st November (All Saints)
11th November (Armistice Day)
Christmas Day

We give below a list of the different sorts of shops, though there is a good deal of overlapping in what they sell. The grocers can sell wine, vegetables and dairy produce, and some cooked meats; the *charcutier* (delicatessen), in addition to cooked meats, may be a pork butcher and poulterer, as well as selling some groceries. Some butchers sell *charcuterie* as well as meat. The *crémerie* is primarily for dairy produce but often branches out into general groceries as well. However, what you don't find in one is bound to be in another, and a good supermarket will keep everything. The chain of 'Casino' supermarkets in the South is good value and stocks many reasonable own-brand goods.

There is very little frozen food so far; the French are conservative about cooking and feel (quite rightly) that there is nothing better than food prepared in their own kitchen. Despite their suspicion of short cuts, a number of freeze-dried 'ready meals' are appearing in the shops, which are quick and easy to make. They make four servings, are not expensive (for France!) and have instructions in English. The range includes *Pizza*, *Quiche Lorraine* (cheese and ham flan), *Couscous* (an Algerian dish of chicken, lamb and vegetables) and *Cassoulet* (casserole of pork and haricot beans).

grocer's	*épicerie*	
	alimentation	
	comestibles	
butcher's	*boucherie*	
cooked meats and	*charcuterie*	There are various
delicatessen shop	*rôtisserie*	combinations of these
poultry and game	*volaille*	
dairy	*crémerie*	
fishmonger's	*poissonnerie*	
greengrocer's	*fruits, primeurs,*	Also available at
	fruiterie	grocer's.
baker's	*boulangerie*	
cakes and pastries	*pâtisserie*	
confectioner's	*confiserie*	

Fish

Fish on the Atlantic and Channel coasts is plentiful and can be cheap, especially some of the smaller shellfish such as mussels (always in season), and clams (*praires*). There is a good variety though the prices fluctuate almost daily, depending on the weather, the demand, the size of boats and catch. The fishmonger will confidently assure you that everything is good and never out of season.

Fishmongers abound in many seaside towns. You can also buy from stalls down by the quayside (the fly population can be rather dense) or choose your shellfish from a *vivier*. There are several *viviers* along the coast of Brittany and even if you don't feel tempted to buy, they are worth a visit. The shellfish are caught and brought from near and far (lobsters from Scotland and Ireland) and left to swim in sea-water pools so that a supply is always on hand, whatever the weather. In smaller places, the *viviers* are only open in the tourist season.

Inland, fishmongers become scarcer; the large towns will certainly boast one or two, sometimes enhanced by a fresh water tank from which you can choose your trout or eel. Smaller towns may not rise to a fish shop at all and, since frozen fish is limited (and not particularly good), you may have to resign yourself to tinned tuna and sardines. The prices will of course be much higher, even for locally-caught fish like the Loire salmon.

In the South of France, prices reach their peak. Most of the fish comes from the West coast in refrigerated lorries. The Mediterranean fish is equally expensive and much of it unexciting in taste, though not in looks. Exceptions are *daurade* (sea-bream), *St. Pierre* (John Dory), *espadon* or *empereur* (swordfish) and fresh sardines and anchovies.

Smoked haddock and kippers are available—the latter come mostly from Fécamp and are sent all over France.

There is usually a price list displayed in the fishmonger's and here are some of the names you will see:

lavaret	lake fish of salmon family
limande	lemon sole
lotte	pout, angler
lotte de mer	angler fish
loup de mer	sea bass
maquereau	mackerel
merlan	whiting
minard	octopus
morue	salt cod
morue fraîche	cod
morue noire	haddock
morue St. Pierre	haddock
moules	mussels
muge	grey mullet
mulet	grey mullet
nonats	like whitebait
ombrine	bar
oursin	sea urchin
pagel	red sea-bream
pagre	sea-bream
palourde	clam
peignes	scallops
perche	perch
pétoncles	scallops
pieuvre	octopus
plie	plaice
poulpe	octopus
praire	clam
rascasse	scorpion fish
raie	skate
rigadelle	clam
rouget	red mullet
royan	like sardine
St. Pierre	John Dory
sardine	sardine
saumon	salmon
sèche	cuttlefish
seiche	cuttlefish
sole	sole
sourdon	cockle
tanche	tench
tenille	clam
thon	tunny, tuna
tourteaux	large crabs
truite	trout
truite de rivière	river trout
truite saumonée	salmon trout
turbot	turbot
vignette	winkles (Brittany)
vignots	winkles (Brittany)
vive	weever

aiglefin	haddock	*crevettes roses*	prawn
aigrefin	haddock		
aiguillat	dogfish	*daurade*	sea-brea
alose	shad	*denté*	gilthead
anchois	anchovy	*dorade*	sea-brea
anguille	eel	*dorée*	John Do
anguille de mer	conger eel		
araignées de		*écrevisse*	crayfish
mer	spider crabs	*églefin*	haddock
		églefin fumé	smoked
bar	bass		haddock
barbeau	barbel	*empereur*	swordfish
bigorneaux	winkles	*encornet*	swordfish
blanchailles	whitebait	*escargots de*	
brelins	winkles (Nor-	*mer*	winkles
	mandy)	*espadon*	swordfish
brème	bream	*esturgeon*	sturgeon
bouffis	kippers		
brochet	pike	*fléon*	clam
brocheton	small pike	*flétan*	halibut
bucardes	cockles	*fruits de mer*	all small
			shellfish
cabillaud	cod		
calmar	squid		
carpe	carp	*gardon*	roach
carpillon	small carp	*goujon*	gudgeon
carrelet	plaice	*goujonnière*	gudgeon
clam	clam (Pro-	*grondin*	gurnet
	vence)	*guignettes*	winkles
clovisse	clam		
colin	hake	*hareng*	herring
congre	conger eel	*hareng fumé*	kipper
coques	cockles	*homard*	lobster
coque rayée	clam	*huîtres*	oyster
coquilles St.	scallops		
Jacques		*lamproie*	lamprey
crabe	crab	*langouste*	crawfish
craquelot	bloater	*langoustines*	scampi, Dubl
crevettes	shrimps		Bay prawns

Meat

As we have already mentioned, meat is incredibly expensive; veal escalopes or steak can set you back nearly £2 per kilo, lamb chops a good £1.50. One is amazed that the French can ever afford to eat meat but, judging by the number of well-stocked butchers' shops full of customers, they evidently do, and probably regard it as a challenge to their ingenuity to produce beautiful sauces to make the meat go further.

It is all home-produced and of excellent quality. It is also all lean, most of the joints being rolled and boned, so at least you are paying for all meat. Pork and some offal are also sold at the *Charcuterie*. The cuts of meat are quite different from British butchers' and are described below. In case you don't feel you can afford a joint, the most economical buys are braising steak (*braiser*), stewing veal (*poitrine de veau*—incidentally, much leaner than in England) and minced steak (*haché* —all good lean meat, no fat or gristle).

The prices of the different cuts must be displayed in the shop. These are most of the names you will see:

BEEF

Roasts	*aloyau de boeuf*	sirloin
	côte de boeuf	rib
	faux-filet	upper part of sirloin, boned
	rosbif	sirloin, boned and rolled
Steaks	*Châteaubrand*	taken from the middle of the fillet
	contrefilet or faux-filet	upper part of sirloin, for rump and T-bone steaks
	entrecôte	similar to Porterhouse
	filet	fillet or undercut
	rumsteck (rumsteak or *romsteck)*	rump steak
	tournedos	small fillet steaks

Stewing	bavette	skirt
	braiser	braising beef
	jarret	shin
	poitrine	brisket
	boeuf haché	minced steak

VEAL

A bit cheaper than lamb and none of it produced by 'factory farming' methods.

Roasts	carré	rib
	épaule	shoulder
	longe	loin
	selle	saddle
Stewing	collier, collet	scrag end of neck
	blanquette	scrag or breast
	jarret	knuckle
	poitrine	breast
Chops etc.	côte	chop
	côtelette	cutlet
	noix	fillet, escalope

LAMB AND MUTTON

Strangely enough, this is the most expensive meat in France, especially leg and shoulder joints and lamb chops. Lamb cutlets and stewing mutton are the cheapest—even then, twice as much as we would pay at home.

Roasts	épaule	shoulder
	épaule d'agneau roulée en ballon	rolled and boned shoulder
	gigot	leg
	selle d'agneau	saddle of lamb
Stewing	basse-côte	breast
	carré de mouton	loin of mutton
	collier, collet	scrag end of neck
	côtelette	cutlet
	côte	chop

Pork

This is also, and in some places only, sold at the *Charcuterie*, together with pork offal, bacon, ham and sausages.

Roasts	*carré*	loin
	cuisse	leg
	échine	spare ribs
	épaule	shoulder, usually rolled and boned
Chops etc.	*côte*	spare rib chop
	côtelette	loin chop
	escalope de porc	fillet
	filet	fillet
	boudin	black pudding, pierced and grilled whole
	crépinette	flat sausages, best bread-crumbed and fried
Sausages	*chair saucisse*	sausage meat
	saucisses	sausages for frying or grilling
	saucisses de Strasbourg	frankfurters
Bacon	*lard*	fat bacon, for adding to casseroles, joints
	poitrine fumée	streaky bacon (pre-packed)
Ham	*jambon de York*	cooked ham
	jambon de Bayonne	raw ham

Poultry

Chicken and game are mostly sold by the *Marchand de Volaille*, although some *Charcutiers* sell cooked and raw chickens and chicken livers.

OFFAL (*Abats*). The following names are the same for all offal
—you just add '*de boeuf*' (beef), '*d'agneau*' (lamb), '*de mouton*'
(mutton), '*de veau*' (veal) and '*de porc*' (pork), e.g. '*rognons de
veau*'—veal kidneys.

abats	offal
cervelle	brains
coeur	heart
foie	liver
gras-double	tripe (3 stomachs of the ox)
langue	tongue
pieds	trotters
queue (*de boeuf*)	(ox)tail
ris	sweetbreads
rognons	kidneys
tripes	tripe (4 stomachs of the ox)

Butchers with a picture or model of a horse's head outside are
called *Boucherie Chevaline* and deal in horse-meat.

The Charcuterie

The *charcuterie* is the most fascinating and fatal of French shops and deserves a chapter to itself. We say 'fatal' because one is rarely strongminded enough to resist the enticing display of food and, though the *charcutier* is happy to serve small amounts, it's all too easy to get carried away in this gourmet's paradise.

A good *charcuterie* keeps all one could need for picnics, salads or quick meals and, though a small shop may only sell cold cooked meats, a selection of *pâté* and things like olives, gherkins and mustard, you will still find delights undreamed of at home. Some *charcuteries* sell pork, others poultry and offal; there is also the combined *boucherie and charcuterie*, which sells all kinds of meat. They all sell lard for cooking (*saindoux*) which is not obtainable at the grocer.

What they do sell falls roughly into five categories:

1. Pâté, cold meats, sausages, etc.
2. Salads and hors d'oeuvres to take away.
3. Savoury pastries and dishes to heat up at home.
4. Spices and flavourings.
5. Fresh meat and poultry (see pp. 19-22).

Some of the food will be easily recognisable but we give below some of the things you might come across for the first time.

PÂTÉ, COLD MEATS, ETC.
Andouilles and Andouillettes (chitterling sausages) may not look very prepossessing but are good sliced, then fried in butter for ten minutes and served with mustard. They make a quick and inexpensive meal with mashed potatoes (the instant kind) or a less plebeian one with chestnut *purée*.

Boudin (black pudding) can also be cooked the same way, for a minute or so longer, or sliced and grilled. Either way, the skin should be pricked with a fork first.

Couennes. A type of brawn, made from pork rinds, with sliced carrots on top—rather rubbery and tasteless, but used by the French to enrich stews.

Jambon de Bayonne. Raw ham, like Parma ham.

Jambonneau. Little conical-shaped cooked hams covered in breadcrumbs. A cheap alternative to slices of cooked ham, but less lean.

Merguèses or Merguez. Algerian sausage—very hot and peppery.

Museau de boeuf. A type of brawn made from the muzzle of beef, sliced in a French dressing with herbs and chopped onions.

Pâté. The variety is endless; some is factory-made but happily the majority of *charcutiers* still make their own. It is sold either in foil, oval china dishes or earthenware terrines (deposit charged on the last two), or more often sliced off a piece the shape of a sandwich loaf. It can be made from duck (*canard*), goose (*oie*), goose or duck's liver (*foie gras*), lark (*alouette*), thrush (*grive*), blackbird (*merle*), hare (*lièvre*), rabbit (*lapin*), pork and veal, with the addition of spices, garlic, brandy or madeira.

Rillettes, Rillons or Rillauds. Similar to pâté, made from pounded pork, rabbit or goose. More spreadable and mushy than a *terrine*. The best ones come from Tours and Le Mans.

Terrine. Another type of pâté—sometimes more chunky and less creamy in consistency. Try a slice with salad and bread, instead of spread on toast *à l'anglaise.*

SALADS AND HORS D'OEUVRES

These are sold by weight, starting at 50 grammes (enough for one) and are ladled into plastic cartons, usually with no lid (as we have discovered to our cost, with vinegar coursing from our shopping basket). In addition to stuffed tomatoes, exciting things in aspic, salads made from cucumber, tomato, beetroot, potato, shredded carrot, artichoke hearts and shellfish, you may find:

Céleri-rave. Celeriac—the bulbous-shaped mild celery, shredded and mixed with mayonnaise. A delicate flavour and very good.

Coeur de palmier. Looks like very thick asparagus stems, in French dressing, and tastes more like artichoke hearts. Should appeal to artichoke fans. One weighs about 50 grammes.

Salade Niçoise. The basic salad should contain anchovies, olives, French beans, tomatoes, pimentos and hard-boiled eggs, but you may find additions, subtractions or variations.

Champignons à la grecque. Mushrooms cooked in oil, water, herbs, spices and lemon juice, served cold. Delicious.

Savoury Pastries and Dishes to Heat Up

For a quick and easy meal to serve with salad or vegetables, these are a boon. If you haven't got an oven, some of them taste just as good cold and these are marked with an asterisk.

*Quiche lorraine.** Either sold by the slice or as individual tartlets, it is a flan made with eggs, cream, bacon and sometimes cheese.

*Barquettes.** Round or boat-shaped pastry cases filled with anything like shellfish, chicken, mushrooms, etc.

*Friands.** Sausage rolls which have considerably more pastry than sausage but are so light they are instantly forgiven. They can also be filled with ham or cheese.

*Allumettes.** Overgrown cheese straws made with puff pastry, more the shape of a Cornish pasty.

*Pizza.** Sold either by the slice or individual-sized ones, it is a flan made from yeast dough, covered with tomato, anchovy, onion, olives and cheese.

Bouchées. Similar to a v*ol au vent,* and usually filled with chicken or shellfish.

Pommes dauphinoises. Mashed potato mixed with *choux* pastry and cheese and deep fried. Sold hot and best eaten straight away.

Couscous. Algerian dish made with chicken, mutton, vegetables, haricot beans and the *couscous* itself—a type of semolina grain which fluffs up when cooked.

Paella. Spanish rice dish, with shellfish and/or chicken, peas and sweet peppers.

Quenelles de brochet. Made from pounded pike, mixed with flour, butter, egg and breadcrumbs, rolled into little sausage-shaped dumplings and poached—ready to be heated up and served with a sauce. They can be exquisite or stodgy and dull, and it's impossible to tell which by looking, but the more expensive ones are the best. They can also be made from chicken —'*quenelles de volaille*'.

Gnocchi. They look like scones draped with shredded coconut, but are in fact made with semolina, egg, milk and cheese and covered with more grated cheese. Warm up in a moderate oven till the cheese melts and starts to bubble.

Coquilles St. Jacques. Scallops in a wine sauce, sometimes with mushrooms or with breadcrumbs on top, ready to heat up in the scallop shell. There are also cold coquilles made with salmon or tunny fish and mayonnaise, but they are expensive and just as easily done at home, even if they don't look quite so alluring without their scallop shells.

SPICES AND FLAVOURINGS
These include different sorts of mustard and pepper, mayonnaise, dried herbs, spices like curry and gherkins, capers and olives. Most of these are also sold at the grocers and a small *charcuterie* may only keep a limited range.

Dairy Produce

MILK is not delivered but is sold at the dairy or grocer. It is all pasteurised and comes in no-deposit plastic bottles of one litre; there are also half-litre bottles and plastic bags in which the milk swishes around in a most alarming fashion while you try to open them—scissors are advisable. Sterilised milk is also available, is slightly more expensive, but will keep for up to ten days in a refrigerator. There is a refundable deposit (*consigne*) charged on glass bottles. In the South of France, the milk looks very watered down—almost blue.

Tins of condensed milk (*lait concentré sucré*) and evaporated milk (*lait concentré non-sucré*) are widely sold. Increasingly popular is powdered instant milk. It comes in packets or large tins and can be added to coffee, used to make hot or cold drinks or made up and used in cooking. It is no cheaper than fresh milk but very convenient. If you prefer it fat-free, ask for it *écrémé*.

BUTTER is all unsalted and costs nearly three times as much as in England, so if you can take any out with you, do.

MARGARINE is less than half the price of butter and the French are using it increasingly for cooking. We've even seen notices in pâtisserie shop windows proclaiming 'all our cakes are made with butter'—a few years ago it would have been unthinkable to make them with anything else.

CREAM is sold in cartons at the *crémerie* and some grocers. It is not expensive, is all double cream and if you are in Normandy or Brittany it may be ladled out of a bowl, a delicious pale yellow with the rich farm cream flavour which one meets all too seldom.

YOGHOURT. To anyone who doesn't like it, the yoghourt sold in France should be a revelation and an invitation to try again.

The non-fruit flavours sold in small foil or plastic cartons with peel-off tops are much more like a mousse and sometimes call themselves *fondant* or *lait gélifié aromatisé*. The varieties include: chocolate (*chocolat*), caramel (*caramel*), coffee (*café*), vanilla (*vanille*), and Grand Marnier.

If you like yoghourt to taste of yoghourt, try plain (*nature*) or fruit-flavoured ones. These include: William pears (*poires William*), peach and redcurrant (*pêche et groseille*), cherry (*cérise*), myrtle [like blackcurrant] (*myrte*), strawberry (*fraise*), raspberry (*framboise*).

There is also fruit-flavoured cream cheese—which sounds odd but in fact tastes very like yoghourt. Among the flavours are: apricot (*abricot*), strawberry (*fraise*), pineapple (*ananas*).

CHEESE
The French have a saying that there is a different cheese for every day of the year; in fact you could almost have two different ones on Sundays because there are around 400 to choose from. Many of them are small or come in their own little box, so you know exactly how much they will cost and don't go through the agony of deciding whether to get 100 or 200 grammes and whether you can afford it anyway. If it's a question of buying a slice off a large cheese, it's probably better to get too little because most of them can't be used for cooking—unlike stale mousetrap!

Cheese is sold in the *crémerie*, grocers and some markets. Nobody minds if you take the lid off and prod to see if it's ripe (*mûr*) and you may even be invited to try a piece if you have never bought it before. (Useful words in this context are *coulant*: runny, and *passé*: over-ripe.)

We are all for trying local cheeses (*fromage du pays*) which you may never see in England or even in France, outside their birthplace. Several are made from goats' milk and some from ewes' and are perfectly delicious. If you don't like the thought of it, don't ask what it's made from. Or try it first, then ask afterwards if you enjoyed it.

For those who like to experiment, we list a few alternatives to the more familiar cheeses imported into Britain, plus the district where they are made or their brand name, in the case of those widely distributed through France.

BLUE-VEINED CHEESES
If you like Roquefort or the stronger Bleu de Bresse, try some of these

Bleu d'Auvergne or Bleu de Salers	Auvergne
Bleu de l'Aveyron	Aveyron
Bleu de Basillac	Limousin
Bleu des Causses	Guyenne
Bleu de Haut-Jura	Jura
Bleu de Laqueville	Auvergne
Fourme d'Ambert or Fourme de Cantal	Auvergne
Gex	Franche-Comté
Grièges	Franche-Comté
Laguiole	Auvergne
Mont-Cenis	Mont-Cenis
Olivet bleu	Orléanais
Persillé de Savoie	Savoy
Pontgibaud	Auvergne
Sassenage	Dauphiné
Septmoncel	Jura
Tignard	Savoy

CAMEMBERT AND BRIE TYPES
Camembert is no longer made only in Normandy, but the place of origin must by law appear on the label. The best Brie is the Brie de Meaux, followed by the Brie de Melun. Both come from the Ile de France and are at their best from October to early June. Other similar cheeses are:

Carré de l'Est	Champagne-Lorraine
Chaource	Champagne
Coulommiers or Brie façon Coulommiers	Ile de France
Decize	Nivernais
Huppemeau	Orléanais
Rollot	Picardy

BLAND CHEESES
These are the mild buttery types, like Bonbel and Port Salut, though some of them (like Maroilles) become stronger when left to ripen.

Beaumont	Savoy
Maroilles	Thiérache
Pont-l'Evêque	Normandy
Port du Salut or Port Salut	Brittany
Providence	Normandy
Reblochon	Savoy
Saint Nectaire	Auvergne
Saint Paulin	Brittany, Lorraine
Tomme au Raisin (covered in grape pips)	Savoy

CREAM CHEESE
In this category come the cheeses eaten as a dessert in France: the fresh cream cheese *fromage blanc* sold in large and small plastic cartons which is eaten with sugar (it can also be eaten with salt but since it's a very simple sour milk cream cheese, this is an acquired taste) and *Petit-suisse*, often sold in tiny foil cartons, six at a time. This is again eaten with sugar and is even better with fresh strawberries or raspberries. It can also be fruit-flavoured.

The delicious double and triple cream cheeses perish quickly and are best bought in small quantities to eat the same day. These include:

Brillat Savarin	Normandy
Boursault and Boursin (either plain or flavoured with herbs and garlic or black pepper)	
Gervais	Normandy
Monsieur Fromage	Normandy
Fontainebleau	Ile de France
Gourmandise (flavoured with kirsch or sometimes hazelnuts)	
Saint-Florentin	Burgundy

GOAT CHEESES

These are more expensive than cows' cheese since there are fewer goats and their milk yield is lower. Many of them are excellent but with age their distinctive tang develops an acidity as overpowering as ammonia, so unless you have an iron constitution, think in terms of days and weeks, rather than months, when choosing a goat cheese. They are usually small and their forms are pretty standard: small ovals, pyramids, cylinders and *crème caramel* shapes. Some are wrapped in chestnut leaves to keep them moist (like Banon) or rolled in ashes (Cendré de Vendôme). Sancerre, Dieux and Rocamadour are pleasant if young but become sour and acid when aged. Le Pouligny and Camembert de Chèvre can be very salty. Among the unusual ones are those flavoured with herbs, such as:

Fenouil	rolled in powdered fennel
Poivre d'Ane	wrapped in savory, similar to wild thyme
Provence	rolled in crushed herbs
Romarin	Rolled in powdered rosemary
Sarriette	rolled in powdered savory

PROCESSED CHEESE

There is little processed cheese, apart from the excellent 'Vache qui Rit' and what there is does not debase itself further by mixing with tomato, celery, etc.

COOKING CHEESE

The most widely used cooking cheese is gruyère and this can be bought ready-grated (*râpé*). There is also, believe it or not, a type of cheddar cheese called 'Chester'.

Vegetables and Fruit

France imports more fruit and vegetables than either Spain or Italy, so there is always a good choice. Equally, they are able to grow more exotic things than we can, like melons, aubergines and peppers, so once these are in season they become cheap.

The standard is high, the goods beautifully displayed and the shopkeepers helpful over choosing peaches that are right for today or a melon for tomorrow night. The seasons for home-grown produce start a fortnight to a month earlier than in England. Nearly everything is sold by weight, so don't be alarmed at the price ticket on a cucumber or melon—it's the price per kilo. One cucumber around 10 inches long weighs around 300 grammes and a Charentais melon (little larger than a grapefruit) under 500 grammes. No-one minds if you just ask for two peaches or three tomatoes. Radishes, asparagus and young carrots and turnips are sold by the bunch (*le paquet* or *la botte*).

Vegetables and fruit from the greengrocer and market will be the freshest and best value. They can also be bought at some grocers and supermarkets.

Most of the fruit and vegetables are a familiar sight at home, so need no description, but here are a few unfamiliar ones you may like to try:

YELLOW RASPBERRIES. A pale, orangey yellow, they are not under-ripe but, if anything, are sweeter and juicier than ordinary raspberries. June and July.

CHARENTAIS MELON. These little melons, enough for two people, come first from the Midi and then the Charente. They are similar to a cantaloup, but sweeter and very juicy.

WILD STRAWBERRIES (*fraises des bois*) are like miniature strawberries. They are slightly more expensive than cultivated ones and are especially good sprinkled with white wine and sugar.

POMEGRANATES (*grenades*). See p. 97 (Spanish section).

MEDLARS or Japanese medlars (*nèfles*). These look a little like crab-apples. They bruise easily and often look rather battered when you buy them. This doesn't seem to affect the flavour. They are juicy but with a slightly drying aftertaste.

CELERIAC (*céleri-rave*). See p. 62 (Italian section).

CHICORY (*endive*) is more readily available in winter and spring and can either be used shredded in salads or sliced lengthwise and braised in butter (a frying pan with a lid will do). Either way, it is excellent.

BEANS (*haricots verts*). There are various sorts of French string beans; the more usual tiny green ones, and the less usual blue and pale yellow ones. These are every bit as good, though the blue ones disappointingly turn green when cooked. There is also a variety called 'Ecosse' and another called 'Mange-tout', looking like flat pea-pods with tiny peas in and, as the name suggests, you eat them, pods and all.

MUSHROOMS (*champignons*). In addition to the cultivated mushroom, there are large edible fungi called *morilles* and *cèpes* (also tinned) and a shrivelled little yellow mushroom called *girolle*. None of them looks very exciting, nor are they cheap, but they have a haunting flavour and a little goes a long way.

CHARD OR WHITE BEET (*blette, bette* or *poirée*). See p. 63 (Italian section).

FLORENCE FENNEL (*fenouil*). Mostly winter and spring. See p. 63 (Italian section).

SALSIFY (*salsifis*), a herb of the chicory family, with a long, edible root. They are very good tinned.

COURGETTES, PEPPERS AND AUBERGINES. See pp. 62, 64 (Italian section).

Tinned fruit and vegetables are very expensive, so if you want a rest from preparing fresh vegetables, take a few tins out with you. Occasionally there is a special offer and if you see a tin of *flageolets* going cheap and if you like the idea of little kidney beans, do try one. We haven't yet seen baked beans or tinned spaghetti. There is not much variety of frozen vegetables or fruit (only strawberries and raspberries), and anyway they are far too dear.

TRUFFLES. Among the numerous varieties, the black truffles are the most highly prized. They are grown in Périgord and the Charente and are on sale everywhere as a much vaunted (and alarmingly expensive) local product. The fresh ones only keep for a week but you can get them tinned, though they lose some of their unique flavour. They are in fact 'a variety of parasitic mushroom which grows on the roots of certain oak and hazel-nut trees' (*Dictionnaire Encyclopédique de l'Epicerie*, by A. Seigneurie, 1904). They are famed for the flavour they add to a dish, rather than how they taste themselves when cooked. If you want to try them without incurring vast expense, buy a slice of pâté 'truffé'—identified by the chopped truffles dotted about like little bits of black boots.

White truffles, with a different but equally haunting flavour, are grown in Italy, in Piedmont. They need hardly any cooking and can be eaten raw, finely sliced, and added to a risotto instead of mushrooms.

SALADS. There is a good choice of salad greenery if you feel like a change from cabbage lettuce (*laitue*) or cos (*romaine*). Endive (confusingly called *chicorée*) comes in two varieties, Batavian (*scarole*) and curly (*chicorée frisée*). The Batavian looks like a plump lettuce, its outer leaves spread out and wavy at the edges. The curly sort is a riot of frilly leaves. It can taste rather sharp so it's a good plan to mix it in with other salad vegetables. It keeps very well in polythene without wilting.

The French eat cultivated dandelion leaves (*pissenlits*). These can be very good, especially with the following dressing: fry some little cubes of streaky bacon till the fat runs; pour this over the salad, add two tablespoons of wine vinegar to the frying pan, and when it is bubbling add it to the salad. Mix well and serve. Endives also can be dressed in this way.

Belgian chicory (confusingly called *endive*) is equally good sliced in rings or lengthwise and served with a dressing made with lemon juice, but don't prepare it too far ahead since, once sliced, it goes brown after a few minutes.

Sorrel (*oseille*) can be cooked like spinach, and makes very good soup.

Bread, Cakes and Biscuits

BREAD. French bread is excellent and cheap. Since all bakers bake once or twice a day, it should always be fresh, crusty and sometimes still warm. However, it goes stale quickly, so if possible buy it every day.

A price list must by law be displayed in the shop and, though the names of the different bread may vary according to the district, the basic sizes of bread are the same. The very large, $1\frac{1}{2}$ kilos and 1.200 grms., can be long or round and squashy like an enormous cottage loaf, but unless you are a large party and can demolish one of these at a sitting it is better to buy the smaller loaves of 500 or 250 grammes. These are called variously *baguette*, *perrosien* or *bâtard*. The very thin long loaf is called *flûte* or *ficelle* and is easiest to spread when sliced lengthwise. Bread rolls are called *petits pains*.

For sandwiches or toast you can buy bread the shape of an English tin loaf called *pain de mie*, either unsliced, sliced (*coupé*) and wrapped, or the baker will slice it for you. It is sometimes sold at the grocers too.

Brown bread (*pain bis* or *pain complet*) is shaped like a sandwich loaf and is also sometimes sold at the grocer's. Rye bread (*pain de seigle*), usually a round loaf, keeps well for several days in a polythene bag. Starch-reduced bread is *pain de régime*. *Biscottes* are sold everywhere.

The baker also bakes *croissants*, the flaky, crescent-shaped rolls, so good for breakfast (even better if warmed), and *brioches*. If the shop is a pâtisserie as well, there will be a mouthwatering selection of cakes and pastries, fruit tartlets, home-made biscuits and any local speciality. If you happen to be in Brittany, you might like to try a slice of the *flan Breton* which is sold everywhere; it is made with a cream and egg-custard filling and raisins. We found the *galettes* and *gâteau Breton* disappointingly dry. Savoury things like sausage rolls are left to the *Charcuterie*. *Pâtisserie* things are as gorgeous as they look, but not cheap, and the French eat them more often for their sweet course. The large cakes are very much party pieces, but it would be worth lashing out just once and trying one. Many have liqueur-flavoured fillings and have 'Cointreau' or 'Grand Marnier' delicately written on them in filigree icing.

CAKES. Cakes more suitable for tea are now being sold pre-packed at the grocer; Swiss rolls (called obscurely *Milady*) with apricot or strawberry jam filling, fruit cake (called *cake*), chocolate and hazelnut cakes, some richer ones with liqueur fillings, and jam tarts. There are some inexpensive cake-mixes (*préparations*) on the market and a good puff pastry mix (*préparation pour la pâte feuilletée*). You can also buy frozen puff pastry and frozen ready-to-bake flan cases (*tarte feuilletée surgelée*) but, though labour saving, they aren't cheap and are only available in large towns.

BISCUITS. Biscuits are excellent, some only marginally dearer than in England. There is also a good selection of savoury and cocktail biscuits. The home-made biscuits and *petits fours* sold at the *pâtisserie* cost much more but are worth it for the occasional treat.

CRÊPES. Breton pancakes, which look like a cross between chamois leather and a doyley, can be bought in packets and either eaten spread with butter and jam or heated up in butter and served like pancakes, although they are much sweeter.

Miscellaneous Groceries

ASPIC JELLY. Only plain gelatine is sold, but made up with stock can be used as aspic.

BABY FOODS. There are jars of strained and junior foods in the most amazing range of flavours. No wonder the French have such discerning palates when from babyhood they are tempted by artichokes, fillet of sole with vegetables, and quince and apple *compote*! There are less exotic varieties too, plus various cereals for mixing with milk. All are available both at grocers and chemists but cost twice as much as in England.

BREAKFAST CEREALS. There is a good range (though no Weetabix type) but they are very expensive and are not stocked everywhere, although they are made in France.

CURRY. Widely available and costs the same as pepper.

GOLDEN SYRUP. Not obtainable.

HONEY (*miel*). Both thick and thin; it's sometimes sold on roadside stalls which proves even more expensive than in the shops.

JAM (*confiture*). All very good, not cheap but with some unusual flavours like melon, peach and pineapple.

JELLIES. There are no fruit jellies but powdered gelatine is sold and this could be mixed with fruit juice.

KETCHUP. Sold everywhere.

MAYONNAISE. Sold at the grocer's and *charcuterie*, either in tubes or jars. Some is lemon-flavoured and it all tastes unsynthetic and home-made.

MARMALADE. Called *confiture d'oranges*. Rather sweet. If you ask for *marmelade*, you will be landed with stewed fruit.

MUSTARD. Sold at the grocer's and *charcuterie*. Not as strong as the English variety, and the darker the mustard, the milder it is. Moutarde de Dijon is made with white wine and tarragon.

OIL. The French are using oil more for cooking, now that butter is so dear. In Provence, much of the traditional cooking involves olive oil. The next cheapest is groundnut oil (*huile d'arachides*), followed by corn oil. (Groundnut oil comes in two qualities: *supérieure* for cooking, and the cheaper *huile de table* used for salads, mayonnaises, etc.) Walnut oil (*huile de noix*), made in Périgord, is rich, strong and an acquired taste—some of our French friends have even suggested that it is only suitable for sewing-machines.

PEPPER (*poivre*), black, white, ground and unground is sold everywhere but costs twice as much as in England.

PASTA. This is reasonable, sold everywhere, and there is a good selection including macaroni, noodles, soup pasta and cannelloni ready for stuffing. No fresh ravioli but plenty of tinned.

PUDDING MIXES. There are several chocolate blancmange types around. Angel mousse needs no cooking—just beat with fresh or evaporated milk. There are also tins of a delicious confection called *crème dessert*, somewhat extravagant but it can be stretched further by adding beaten egg white. Some of the flavours are chocolate, coffee, vanilla, Grand Marnier, caramel and praline (hazel nuts).

RICE. The round grain rice for puddings is *riz Caroline* and the Patna rice called *grain long*. Semolina and tapioca are also widely sold.

SALT. There are various grades of salt, in varying degrees of coarseness: *sel de table, sel raffiné, sel gemme* (rock salt), *sel marin* (sea salt for grinding in a salt mill) and *gros sel* or *sel gris*, the coarsest of all.

SUGAR (*sucre*). Granulated, caster, icing and lump sugar are all widely sold. Brown sugar (*cassonade*) is not much used in France and is only stocked by the larger grocers' shops.

VINEGAR. The most ubiquitous is *vinaigre coloré*, a pinkish colour and much milder than malt vinegar. Red and white wine vinegar are a little dearer but better. You can also buy vinegar flavoured with tarragon or shallots, both good for salad dressings. The latter is used in France sprinkled on oysters.

Beverages and Soft Drinks

TEA can be bought anywhere, in packets or tea bags. Ignore the packets inscribed *tilleul, menthe* or *verveine* unless you want an infusion of lime, mint or verbena.

COFFEE is much less expensive than instant coffee. This costs twice as much as in England, though there is a much cheaper coffee and chicory mixture, every bit as good.

COCOA is sold everywhere, usually unsweetened. Chocolate-flavoured 'Nesquik' is widely sold—so far, no other flavours.

MINERAL WATER is sold everywhere—grocer, wine merchant, chemist. Both the still and fizzy sorts have *eau minérale naturelle* on the label, but the fizzy is marked *gazeuse* as well. The bottles, large or small, carry a deposit.

FRUIT DRINKS. These are all expensive, so take as much as you can with you. However, if you run out or haven't room, there are a few alternatives. As in Spain and Italy, there is no equivalent of squash, though there are a number of syrups (*sirops*) for diluting with water, mineral water or fizzy lemonade. The flavours include orange, lemon, grapefruit, strawberry, *grenadine* (made from pomegranates) and *cassis* (blackcurrant)—this is similar to Ribena. They are all terribly sweet—probably too much even for the British palate, despite our reputation as the world's leading guzzlers. It helps if you add lemonade or a squeeze of fresh lemon. The tinned concentrated syrups by Teisseire, though expensive, last longer and are popular with children.

FRUIT JUICE comes in tins (very expensive) and little bottles (ditto). The apricot, in particular, is as thick as liquidised fruit so can be diluted a little. There are also litre bottles of ready diluted orange, lemon, grenadine, grape and apple juice. These are less sweet—the grape pleasantly tangy, but the apple reminiscent of flat cider and stewed apples. These bottles carry a deposit and if you are travelling try and return the empties where you bought them, since shops in other areas may refuse to accept them.

FIZZY DRINKS are mostly sold in litre bottles, with a deposit— the usual variety of orange, lemon, lemonade and Coca-Cola, none of them cheap.

Tonic water and soda (*Perrier*) are widely sold, but not bitter lemon.

Wines and Spirits

Wines and spirits are sold at grocers', supermarkets and wine merchants' (*marchands de vin*). Most cafés and bars would oblige with a bottle of brandy or Dubonnet, though they are less likely to sell wine, except by the glass.

A fair amount of French wine is a familiar sight to us in the shops at home, though it may come as a rude shock to find that good wines are only slightly less expensive in France than in Britain. However, for every day there are plenty of reasonable *vins ordinaires*. Steer clear of any red less than 12 degrees of alcohol and any white less than 11 degrees.

Over three million acres in France are dedicated to producing wine, so you may easily discover a local *vin du pays* where you are staying, that costs little more than a brand-named *vin ordinaire*, and has much more character. We list below the main wine-growing areas of France:

Burgundy and Lower Burgundy
Chalonnais, Mâconnais and Beaujolais
Nivernais and Berry
Central Plateau
Côtes-du-Rhône
Alps
Provence
Languedoc-Roussillon
Bordeaux
Dordogne, Tarn, Lot
Lot, Aveyron, Lozère
Tarn, Haute-Garonne, Ariège
Pyrenees and Landes
Nantes and Brittany
Anjou
Touraine
Franche-Comté
Alsace

Algeria and Corsica also produce wine. Much of the Algerian is coarse and used for blending, though some is exported to France for table wines. However, it seems a waste to try it when there is such an enormous choice of French wine. The Corsican wine travels badly, so is little known outside Corsica.

BRANDY. Once again, French brandy is familiar to us, though there are several makes that are not exported. Good brandy is slightly less expensive than in England but the cheaper brands cost under £2 per bottle. Liqueurs are 10-20 per cent cheaper and usually even small shops stock a good range. *Marc, eau-de-vie* made from grape pressings, is produced in every wine-growing area but varies considerably in quality.

GIN AND WHISKY are sold in the larger shops at about the same price as in England, though some Scotch whisky costs half as much again.

APÉRITIFS. There is a good choice of wine-based apéritifs, reasonably priced. The very cheap ones tend to be insipid. Several are sweetish, similar to Dubonnet or white Cinzano, like St. Raphael and Ambassadeur. If you like the aniseedy sort, such as Pernod, there are Ricard, Pastis and Berger as well.

CIDER comes from Brittany and Normandy. It is sold in litre bottles and can be either flat (*plat*) or fizzy (*mousseux*); the latter tastes more like English cider.

BEER is all of the light continental type.

CHAMPAGNE is expensive, even the non-vintage. Sparkling Vouvray makes an acceptable, cheap alternative.

ITALY

General

Housekeeping costs should be, on balance, about the same as in England since cheaper vegetables, fruit, cheese and some fish compensate for dearer butter and meat. Rice and pasta (spaghetti, etc.) are cheap and easy to cook and, followed by salad and fresh fruit, make good holiday meals.

Cooking with butter is not economical, so the Italians use oil. Olive oil is surprisingly expensive and is kept for salads, though the cheaper *olio di semi* is a good substitute and widely used for cooking. Made from sunflower seeds, it is tasteless, has no smell and is excellent value.

Shopping can be a pleasure. Shopkeepers expect you to take an interest in what you are buying and to choose carefully. Nobody is offended if you handle the food and it is quite normal to pick up a fish and gaze into its eyes to see that it is fresh.

Hours, too, are convenient: shops open at 8 or 8.30 a.m., shut for two or three hours at lunch time and then stay open until 8 or 9 p.m. On Sundays they open from 8.30 a.m. until lunchtime. In the north, the lunch-hour is shorter and shops close earlier.

There is an ever-increasing number of supermarkets; the Standa and Co-operative chains are very good. Large towns have food markets open every day, and in the smaller towns they are open once or twice a week.

The most useful shops to recognise are:

general groceries	*alimentari*
greengrocer's	*frutta e verdura*
all dairy produce, some groceries	*latteria*
baker's	*panetteria*
cakes and pastries	*pasticceria*
fishmonger's	*pescheria*
poultry	*polleria*
cooked chickens to take away	*pollo allo Spiedo*
meat, some poultry and game	*macelleria*

cold and hot cooked meat, roasted on the premises	*rosticceria*
delicatessen	*salumeria*
vegetables and herbs	*verdure, erbe*
wines and spirits	*vini e liquori*

One important point is that salt can only be bought in a tobacconist's shop; its sale is controlled by the Government.

National holidays, when all the shops and banks are shut, are apt to crop up without any warning. These are:

New Year's Day	
6th January	Epiphany
19th March	St. Joseph
Good Friday and Easter Monday	
25th April	Liberation Day
1st May	Labour Day
6th Thursday after Easter	Ascension Day
2nd June	Proclamation of the Republic
1st Thursday after Trinity	Corpus Christi
29th June	St. Peter and St. Paul
15th August	Assumption
1st November	All Saints' Day
4th November	Victory Day, 1918
8th December	Conception of the Virgin
Christmas and Boxing Day	

There are various local *Festa* days, held in honour of the towns' Patron Saints. The main ones are:

25th April	St. Mark	Venice
24th June	St. John the Baptist	Florence, Genoa and Turin
19th September	St. Gennaro	Naples
4th October	St. Petronio	Bologna
7th December	St. Ambrose	Milan

If any of these Festa days occur during your holiday, make a note in your diary beforehand so that you're not caught on the hop with no food or money.

Kitchens in Italian flats are pretty well equipped. All cooking is done by Butane gas. Ovens can be regulated, but they don't have grills. A ridged frying pan is often used instead, imprinting lines on the fish or meat so that it looks as if it's been grilled by charcoal. Only about half the kitchens run to teapots and kettles (more likely if the property is let through a British agency), so if tea is an indispensable part of your holiday you may need to take a teapot with you and your own tea—you can buy it there but it's more expensive.

Fish

There is a good range of fresh fish which can be bought from fishmongers or in fish markets on the coast. Some are found only on the Adriatic (like sturgeon), some only on the Mediterranean; the fish common to both seas are often sold under different names. Half the names scrawled on slates are no help in identifying them, either because of defective spelling or dialects, and those that are given in dictionaries have such alarming translations like 'miller's thumb' and 'dragon weever' that it's better not to think of the English equivalent but just accept them as they are.

The Mediterranean fish vary from picturesque to frankly repulsive to look at. Many do not taste very exciting and need livening up with onions and tomatoes, herbs or sauces.

Some are certainly worth trying, like sea-bass (known variously as *spìgola*, *spinola* or *branzino*), the angler or frog fish (*rana pescatrice*, *rospo* or *boldro*), bar (*ombrina*), members of the sea-bream family (*orata*, *dorata*, *sparo*, *dèntice* and *boga*), sword fish (*pesce spada*), John Dory (*Sampietro*) and fresh tunny (*tonno* or *vitello di mare*). For grilling or if you have a barbecue, try *dèntice*, red mullet (*triglie*) and grey mullet (*muggine* or *cèfalo*). Small fish suitable for dipping in flour and frying in oil are fresh sardines, anchovies (*acciughe* or *alici*) and a substitute for whitebait (*pesciolini*). The Italians also fry these in batter, together with small red mullet, prawns and squid or inkfish; served with lemon quarters, this *fritto misto* is very good.

Fishmongers are usually most obliging about cleaning fish or shelling scampi (though the weight of the shells is included in the price). Often the fish will be hidden away from marauding flies, so if the shop looks bare, it doesn't mean it's sold out.

A number of freshwater fish make good eating, such as carp (*carpione*—trout family), perch, trout and *agoni* (shad from the Lombardy lakes).

Fresh shellfish. Every sort of shellfish is available, though much of it is fiddly to prepare on holiday. *Gamberoni*, giant prawns, can be grilled with their shells on. *Tartufi di mare* or *caparozzoli* a kind of cockle) are eaten raw. *Moleche*, soft-shelled crabs from Venice, are caught in April and May; they can be dipped in batter—claws and all—and fried in boiling oil. If you can bear the thought of such infanticide, you will find them delicious.

Scampi and crayfish (*aragosta*) can just be boiled in salted water and served hot with melted butter or left to get cold in the pan and served with mayonnaise.

The fresh mussels and clams are so good that if you have the time to prepare them, they are well worth the trouble. (See recipes p. 123.)

Frozen fish. This includes halibut, hake, perch, and *dèntice*, *ombrina*, a mixed fish for frying, a delicious fish soup-cum-stew (*Zuppa di pesce*), fish cakes and fish fingers. These last taste much more strongly of fish than English ones.

Tinned fish. Salmon and tuna fish are good and reasonably priced. There are several types of shellfish, including *vòngole* (little clams), especially good in a sauce made with oil, garlic, herbs and tomatoes and served with spaghetti.

Some of the fish you may want to buy are listed below:

acciughe	anchovies	*calamari*	squid, cuttle-fish
agone	shad		fish
alborelle	bleaks	*calcinnelli*	clams
alici	anchovies	*canestrelli*	scallops
alosa	shad	*cappe*	clams
anguilla	eel	*carpione*	carp
aragosta	crayfish	*cèfalo*	grey mullet
aringa	herring	*cernia*	stone bass
arselle	clams	*cheppia*	shad
astaco	lobster	*coda di rospo*	angler tail
		conchiglie dei	
baccalà	dried salt cod	*pellegrini*	scallops
bastoncini di		*coregone*	lake whitefish,
pesce	fish fingers		salmon
bianchetti	whitebait		family

branzino	sea bass	*cozze*	mussels
cuori di mare	cockles	*peoci*	mussels (Venetian name)
dèntice	gilthead, sea-bream	*pesce cappone*	gurnard, gurnet
gamberetti grigi	shrimps	*pesce persico*	perch
		pesce spada	swordfish
gamberetti rosi	prawns	*pescatrice*	angler, frog fish
gamberi	crayfish	*pettini*	scallops
grancevole	spider crabs	*polpo*	octopus
granchi	crabs	*polipetto*	small octopus (Genoese)
grongo	conger eel		
ippoglosso	halibut	*rana pescatrice*	frog fish
		razza	skate
limanda	lemon sole	*ricci di mare*	sea urchins
luccio	pike	*rombo*	turbot
merlano	whiting	*salmone*	salmon
merluzzo	hake, cod	*sampietro*	John Dory
mitili	mussels	*sarde*	sprats
molecche	soft-shelled crabs	*sardine*	sardines
moscardini	small squid (Spring only)	*scampi*	scampi, Adriatic, 'Dublin Bay prawns', bigger than our scampi
muggine	grey mullet		
murena	moray		
naselle	hake	*scòrfano*	scorpion-fish, including rascasse
		scòrpena	
ombrina	bar		
orata	gilt head, sea bream	*seppie*	cuttle fish, squid
ostriche	oysters	*sgombro*	mackerel
		sogliola	sole
pagello	red sea bream	*spìgola*	sea-bass
pagro	sea bream	*stoccafisso*	dried salt cod

passera	flounder	*storione*	sturgeon
tartufi di mare	clams, like	*tetani*	squid
	French	*triglia*	red mullet
	praires	*trota*	trout
tèmolo	grayling	*trota di vivaio*	trout from fish
tinca	tench		tank
tonno	tunny fish, tuna	*vòngole*	clams

Meat

Italian meat may seem expensive but it is all lean and lots of useless fat and bones aren't included in the weight you pay for. The butchers' shops undergo regular and rigorous government inspections for hygiene. The butchers are generally very obliging and will cut your escalope, chop or steak to the required thickness and will bash your veal for you.

There is a good variety of meat and poultry in the larger towns but in the poorer areas the choice is more limited. Some meat is imported from France, Yugoslavia and Argentina.

BEEF AND VEAL. There is a lot of veal and *vitellone* which is sold to be cooked like beef but is best described as teen-age veal. Because of limited grazing, it is too expensive to rear cattle for beef so they are slaughtered younger—half-way between the veal and steak stage, neither a baby nor a grown-up.

Veal used for stewing is expensive and needs long, slow cooking. Chops are cheaper and escalopes cheaper still but vary in quality. It is sometimes sold for joints as *spalla senza osso* (boneless shoulder) or *rotolo*, rolled up and stuffed with herbs. This is inexpensive and delicious but needs long slow cooking.

Vitellone is darker pink than veal but paler than beef. It is sold for stewing and is cheaper than veal. Fillet steak is dearer than rump but unless you've got a really reliable butcher, eating steak in good restaurants is less hit or miss than buying it. The little steaks called *pizzaiola* can be tough and are improved by being fried lightly in butter, then braised in tinned tomatoes sieved through the *mouli*, with a pinch of herbs and seasoning. A good joint for quick cooking is *rosbif* (rolled sirloin), cooked in the oven and covered with finely sliced vegetables.

bistecca	steak
bistecca di filetto	fillet steak
carne tritata	mince
coda di bue	oxtail

controfiletto	sirloin of beef
costata di manzo	sirloin steak
costoletta di vitello	veal chop
fesa di vitello	stewing veal
lingua di bue	ox tongue
lingua salmistrata	salt ox tongue
lombata di bue	sirloin of beef
manzo	beef
petto di vitello	breast of veal
piccata	slices of veal, little escalopes
rosbif or roastbeef	sirloin
scaloppina di vitello	veal escalope
spezzatino di vitello	stewing veal
vitello	veal
vitellone	'teen-age veal', half-way between veal and beef

LAMB is good but expensive.

agnello	lamb
cosciotto d'agnello	leg of lamb
costoletta d'agnello	lamb chop, cutlet
sella d'agnello	saddle of lamb
spalla d'agnello	shoulder of lamb
spezzatino d'agnello	stewing lamb

PORK. This is also dear, though of good quality.

Ham, raw and cooked, is sold everywhere; the cooked is cheaper. Raw smoked ham can be used instead of bacon, which tends to be fat, though it is cheap. Parma ham makes an exquisite *hors d'oeuvres*, eaten raw, cut in very thin slices and served with melon or fresh figs.

Sausages are rather salty and spicy and need a lot of cooking. Some have to be boiled. Frankfurters, tinned and in packets, can be bought, but if you are going to miss a good old English sausage, take tinned ones.

Cold cooked meats, sliced from a joint, are sold at the *rosticceria*. Some supermarkets sell a limited amount at the delicatessen counter. There is not much variety in the way of cold meats and *charcuterie*. *Salame di Parigi* is a type of luncheon meat but the other sorts of salami sausages are numerous. They are basically made from pork, seasoning, herbs and garlic in varying strengths. The home made ones are coarser but the majority sold are factory produced. If you haven't tried any before, say you don't like a strong one: *Non mi piace forte*. *Mortadella* is a much larger salami, cut in paper-thin slices. Pale pink with white blotches, punctuated by whole peppercorns, it has garlicky after-effects but is delicious either in an *hors d'oeuvres* or with ham and salad.

braciola di maiale	pork chop, cutlet
carre di maiale	ribs, loin of pork
costoletta di maiale	pork chop
lombata di maiale	loin of pork
maiale	pork
pancetta affumicata	bacon
prosciutto affumicata	smoked ham
prosciutto cotto	cooked ham
prosciutto crudo	raw ham
prosciutto di Parma	Parma ham
wurstel	frankfurters

POULTRY. Chicken is reasonable and sold either whole, jointed or boned. Stewing chicken seems dearer than roasting, but then you are not paying for the weight of the carcass. Chicken and chicken livers are sometimes sold only by the *pollaiuolo* (the poulterer, who also sells ready-cooked joints), but some butchers keep poultry as well as meat.

RABBIT, surprisingly, costs more than duck.

OFFAL. Calf's liver and kidneys are good, but cost about twice as much as in England.

animelle	sweetbreads
cervelli di vitello	calf's brains
fegato di vitello	calf's liver
frattiglie	offal
rognone di vitello	calf's kidney

Dairy Produce

MILK. There are eight different types of milk; two of these are fresh (skimmed and unskimmed) and the rest form every combination and permutation of homogenised, pasteurised and vitaminised you can think of. None of it is delivered. The fresh milk is bought from the *latteria*, where you take your own bottle to be filled from the churn. It is cheaper but, unless you have good refrigeration facilities, will go off much more quickly. The sterilised milk comes in bottles and cartons like lopsided pyramids and is bought from the grocer or dairy. The cartons are disposable, which is about all they are fit for once one has wrestled to open them.

The various varieties of milk taste like diluted condensed milk, a flavour which is hard to disguise. Tinned condensed and evaporated milk can also be bought, but not instant powdered milk. The condensed milk is not suitable for babies but there are various brands of dried milk for babies on the market.

CREAM can be bought from the *latteria, pasticceria* (cake shop) and some supermarkets keep it heavily refrigerated in small sausage-shaped packs.

BUTTER is unsalted and expensive. It varies considerably in price and is all home produced.

MARGARINE is less than half the price of butter.

YOGHOURT. The variety of flavours does not seem to be large; some shops only stock natural, which is also the cheapest. The fruit flavours have a much sharper taste than English yoghourt and their tartness is refreshing. The fruit is puréed, not whole or in little pieces, and really tastes of the picture on the carton. The flavours are banana, bilberry (*mirtillo*), apricot (*albicocca*), prune (*prugna*), apple (*mela*), raspberry (*lampone*), strawberry (*fresa*) and malt (*kniepp*) which tastes more like coffee. It tends to be runny, and removing the top without getting sprayed is quite a challenge.

CHEESE. Quite a few Italian cheeses find their way into English shops. The most popular are Gorgonzola, Dolcelatte, Bel Paese and Parmesan. Although we are all in favour of trying new food when abroad, these cheeses are well worth eating in their natural habitat; they taste far better and fresher than they do at home.

Cheeses fall into four categories, blue cheese, fresh cheese, bland cheese and processed cheese, together with non-Italian cheeses and *grana* (Parmesan) cheese.

BLUE CHEESE
Gorgonzola, the best known of the blue-veined cheeses, is quite delicious, rich and creamy. Too often in England it has become hard and dry, wrapped in cellophane in a supermarket's refrigerator.

Dolcelatte is milder and even creamier than Gorgonzola.

Moncenisio and *Erbo* are similar to Gorgonzola.

FRESH CHEESE
Most of these can be bought in small sizes if there are only one or two in the family who like them, since they need to be eaten as fresh as possible. Left in the fridge, their delicate flavour vanishes. Some of them, however, are delicious heated to melting point on toast or on a pizza.

Mozzarella, originally made only from buffaloes' milk, is now made mostly from cows' milk. If you have an irresistible urge to try the buffalo, look for *Bufala Garantita* on the label. The small ones arrive tied up in paper, like a scarf going under your chin and knotted on top of your head. Having disentangled the rather soggy knot, be prepared for a gush of whey when you first insert your knife. The consistency is soft and springy and the taste like cottage cheese, only more so. Delicious cooked on pizza.

Mascarpone or mascherpone, a thick cream cheese, with the consistency of a petit-suisse but a flavour more like cottage cheese. It can be treated like clotted cream and eaten with strawberries, or like a Petit-Suisse and eaten with sugar. It can

also be used to make a mousse as follows: take six eggs and
separate the yolks from the whites. Beat the yolks with six
dessertspoons sugar, adding six tablespoons Mascarpone and
six tablespoons cream. Now beat the egg whites and fold them
into the cheese mixture. Leave in the fridge to chill. Cocoa,
brandy or a liqueur may be added before folding in the egg
whites. If you want to vary the quantity it is always one spoonful
cheese, sugar and cream per egg.

Ricotta, made from the whey of ewes' milk, can also be eaten
with sugar. It is like a smooth, creamy cottage cheese and can
be used for pasta dishes (*lasagne, cannelloni*) and for a creamy
filling for puddings and pastries.

Stracchino, a mild cheese which spreads like butter. It has a
noticeably stronger taste when bought in the small sized packs;
if you buy it as a slice off a large *stracchino* the tartness is lost,
and the flavour diminishes to imperceptibility the longer the
large cheese is left to languish in the fridge.

Scamorza, similar in taste and texture to Mozzarella. It comes
in large and small sizes, is yellow and oval shaped. Like Mozzarella, it is sometimes smoked.

Cremino, like our cream cheese, is sold in silver foil wrappers,
under various brand names.

BLAND CHEESE
Bel Paese, the best known, similar in consistency to the Dutch
Gouda or Edam but with a delicious soft flavour. It is made near
Milan by the now famous Italian cheese-making firm, Galbani,
and the quality is first class. It keeps well, though it needs to be
covered, since the outside will harden. *Pastorella*, *Bick* and *Fior
d'Alpe* are similar but not quite as good.

Fontina d'Aosta or *Fontina Valdostana*, made in the Valley
of Aosta, is delicious and a cheese that should appeal to nearly
everyone. Not too strong, the texture of a creamy Caerphilly
and the taste of a combination of Gruyère, Emmenthal and Port
Salut, if such a thing is possible. Far better to taste it and find
out. It is also a good melting cheese and is used for an Italian
version of the Swiss fondue.

Provolone, made in various oval shaped sizes. In its unsmoked
form it is like a mild Dutch cheese. Smoked (*affumicato*), it

ranges from very sharp and salty to the pleasant tang associated with Austrian smoked cheese.

Taleggio, is in fact a Stracchino that has advanced from fresh white innocence to mellow middle age. It has been matured in natural caves for at least forty days, developing a rosy crust outside and a firmer, fuller cheese inside. It should not be allowed to progress further to the ripe Camembert stage; by then, it will be past its prime—verging on senility.

PROCESSED CHEESE

Comes in as many shapes and sizes as in England and tastes exactly the same. Apart from various cheese flavours (Gruyère, Bel Paese), they don't go in for celery, tomato, shrimp etc. additives.

NON-ITALIAN CHEESE

The most ubiquitous are Emmenthal (*Emental*), Gruyère (*Groviera*), Roquefort and Camembert.

GRANA CHEESE

The two cheeses in this category are Grana Padano and Parmesan (Parmigiano), the uniquely flavoured cooking cheese. Its quality is uniformly good and the younger, whiter cheese is good for eating as a table cheese. When buying it for cooking, avoid the pre-packed variety and have it freshly grated. A well-matured cheese should be pale yellow and, though it may have a few white bruise marks, it should not be dried-out and chalky.

Grana Padano can be as good as Parmesan, but the quality is less reliable.

Vegetables and Fruit

The Italians rely much more on home produce and less on imported food than we do; consequently vegetables and fruit tend to be seasonal though, because of the climate, the seasons start earlier and last longer. We take for granted winter lettuce and tomatoes—even if the latter do have a distinctly musty aroma—but the Italians can eat delicious firm tomatoes, fresh from Sicily, as early as April, and asparagus in March.

To supplement the choice of winter vegetables, some summer and autumn produce is bottled (like green beans and artichokes) and pickled. Pickles include tiny mushrooms, artichokes, aubergines, peppers and a mixture called *giardiniera*, made of chopped carrots, cauliflower, peppers, onions and celery. They are preserved in mild vinegar and can be used in *hors d'oeuvres* or with cold meats and salad. Their sharpness has the same astringent effect as curry does in hot weather.

Tinned vegetables are expensive and baked beans are *not* among them. For something typically Italian, *peperonata* is worth a try. It is similar to the Provençal *ratatouille* but is basically a mixture of tomatoes, onion, squash (baby marrow), green and red peppers, and is eaten cold. It could equally be added to a chicken casserole.

There is a good range of frozen vegetables, chiefly by Findus, marginally more expensive than in England. These include most of the ones available here—peas, beans, spinach etc.—and a specially prepared collection, minutely diced to go into soup; there are also green and red peppers, which open up all sorts of exciting possibilities. Corn on the cob and sweetcorn are only available in very tourist-conscious areas.

Throughout the spring and summer, vegetables are plentiful. In some resorts the prices go up in the season so it is cheaper to shop in large towns. The produce will also be fresher in a market than in a shop, though the stalls may be more heavily populated with flies. Either way, vegetables should be washed. If you feel very strongly about precautions when abroad, you can buy crystals of permanganate of potash in England to take with you. A tiny amount turns the water a ravishing purple and when the vegetables or fruit have been washed in this they should be safer than safe.

It is certainly cheaper to buy fresh vegetables, though one naturally doesn't want to spend the entire holiday shelling and peeling. However, aubergines, peppers, artichokes and courgettes are all labour-saving and infinitely more delicious than tinned peas.

A few of the fresh vegetables deserve special mention. Some of them seldom come to England and the ones that do are often regarded with deep suspicion by the British shopper.

GLOBE ARTICHOKES are available all the year round and get bigger as the summer progresses (in Southern Italy there is a large variety called *cardi*). When tiny, they are delicious dipped in batter and fried whole in hot oil. When larger, they need to be cooked in boiling water for about 20 minutes or until the leaves come away easily, and either eaten hot with melted butter or cold with mayonnaise or a vinaigrette dressing. Either way, the stalk and thick leaves at the base are removed first, then the remaining leaves are pulled out one by one, the non-spiky ends dipped in the butter or dressing, then chewed. The delicate flavour is only surpassed by that of the artichoke heart. This is reached when as many leaves as possible have been removed and savoured, to reveal a dome of shredded fibres called the choke. Slice this away at its base and underneath is the heart—only a few mouthfuls of bliss, but worth the hard labour. Tinned or frozen artichoke hearts are excellent in salads.

AUBERGINES, or eggplant, look like diminutive policemen's truncheons, in glossy purply black, or slightly plumper with pale mauve and green streaks. They are available as early as mid-April and become cheaper later in the summer. Various recipes include them on pp. 133, 149, 150.

CELERIAC is a turnip-shaped root, like celery but much harder. The taste is more subtle, and it is particularly good grated or cut into matchstick-strips (after being blanched for a few minutes in boiling water) and mixed with mayonnaise—a mild one because too much vinegar hides the delicate flavour.

CELERY needs no description, except that there are two types: *sedano bianco* for eating raw and *sedano verde* for cooking. *Verde* is available all the year round, *bianco* only in the summer.

CHARD looks like large spinach with thick stems. The stems can be cooked separately and are very good. The leaf part is cooked like spinach and tastes similar, but less bitter.

FLORENCE FENNEL has the same feathery leaves as the herb fennel used for flavouring fish, but it is the bulbous root that is eaten. Like celery, it is made of crisp ridged sticks, but these are wider at the base and taper upward, ending in the feathery bits, which are chopped off when you buy it. A pleasant smell of aniseed assails you, and when the heart of the fennel is eaten raw, thinly sliced in a mixed salad, it has the taste of aniseed too, which curiously enough is a complementary addition to other salad flavours. When cooked it becomes more like celery; it is delicious braised and then covered with grated cheese and browned in a hot oven.

MUSHROOMS. If you can't track down fresh mushrooms, dried ones can be bought in most grocers'. They come in packets, look dark brown, shrivelled and sinister, like something out of a witch doctor's surgery. They need to be soaked for at least an hour in tepid water before use. They taste very definitely of mushroom and are good in a *risotto* or casserole, less good in an omelette.

ONIONS are dark mauve in the winter, till May, but taste just the same as the normal summer ones. Salad onions are broader than English ones.

RADISHES. In some parts of Italy they are black or white as well as red. They are generally larger than English radishes, but beware the bunches of *erbetti*, which look like large radishes and are in fact white beetroot.

COURGETTES, or squash, the miniature marrows, can be cooked in many ways and are plentiful and cheap. Anyone who has a rooted aversion to marrow can be assured that they bear no resemblance to the watery, stringy, tasteless heaps sometimes met in England. The flowers can also be eaten fried. If you are a marrow lover you can buy the big sort too.

TOMATOES come in varying stages of ripeness and the most tortuous shapes. The orange and green ones are excellent in salads, even though they do look under-ripe. The long 'Cirio' variety are good for stuffing.

PEPPERS, like tall, shiny, green tomatoes, are in fact hollow inside except for a few easily removable seeds. They are very good stuffed and baked, added to a stew, or raw, cut up in strips and added to a salad. Crisp, yet juicy and not too hot. They turn orange, then red, as they get riper and are edible at all stages. Tinned red peppers taste quite different (rather as tinned and fresh peaches differ) but equally good. They are soft but just as good in a salad, in omelettes or in risotto.

FRUIT. Practically all the fruit is home-grown. Early strawberries are imported from France and grapefruit from Jaffa, (which is strange when they grow such delicious oranges in Sicily). Apples tend to be cotton-woolly, which is the way Italians like them, so if you prefer a crisp eating apple ask for them *aspre*. They are available all the year round, together with oranges, lemons, pears and bananas. Pears also are cotton-woolly in the winter, but not in summer.

In May there are medlars, cherries (till August), grapes (till Christmas) and strawberries (till July). In June plums and apricots appear; in July peaches (till August) and figs (till September); in August and September melons, persimmons[1] (till Christmas) and pomegranates.

Fruit is sold by weight rather than '4 oranges for a shilling'. Grapefruit can look disconcertingly cheap until you find the

---

[1] The American date-plum.

advertised price is per *etto* (100 grammes) and one grapefruit weighs nearly 400 grammes.

Tinned and frozen fruit is expensive. Frozen bilberries are delicious with ice cream—rather like blackcurrants. Dried prunes can be bought.

As with vegetables, it is advisable to wash all fruit before eating. Fruit ripens quickly in a hot climate, so if it's not to be eaten immediately it's less wasteful to buy it on the under-ripe side. Over-ripe melons can cause upsets!

Bread, Cakes and Biscuits

BREAD. Italian bread is sadly disappointing. It is better to buy little and often because it goes stale very quickly. A lot of it is coarse and rubbery to start with, so by the time it is a few hours old it is quite inedible. It does vary from region to region, as does the shape of the loaf. Some are flat and round, some long like French loaves, and some oblong like English bread. It is possible to find sliced and wrapped loaves.

The best bet are the little rolls (*panini*) which can be delicious. There are three types: *al burro* (made with butter), *al olio* (with oil) and *all' aqua* (with water). The butter ones are best, the water ones can be unpleasantly dry and crumbly.

There is black bread (*pane nero*) and wholemeal bread (*pane integrale*). If you are calorie conscious, you can even buy imported Ryvita, in the more emancipated areas. *Grissini* (breadsticks) are available everywhere.

Alas, there are no exquisite French *croissants* to be found. A *croissant*-shaped impostor called, confusingly, a *brioche* is in no way a substitute. It tastes something like a *brioche*, but only an imitation.

Pan frutto is similar to a fruit and malt loaf. Children like it spread with butter.

BISCUITS. Packets of biscuits of every description can be bought, including easily identifiable types like wafers, crackers, digestive, Marie and assortments of sweet biscuits.

Biscottati, like the French *biscottes*, are a cross between melba toast and rusks. They are either round or the shape and size of a slice of Hovis, salted or unsalted. They make a good substitute for toast (if you haven't a grill) when spread with butter, marmalade, jam, *pâté* etc. but they are less useful for snacks on toast. If you put scrambled egg on top of them they go soggy, and if you serve them side by side, one stab with the knife and fork is enough to scatter bits of brittle *biscottate* in all directions.

The most satisfactory substitute for 'snacks' toast is fried bread. The oblong loaves are easiest—*pane di tost or pane americano*.

CAKES. The cake shops—*pasticcerie*—are full of the most appetising little cakes and pastries. Large cakes are more often beautifully decorated party pieces and are expensive.

Little cakes (*pasticcini*) are cheap and quite good. The chocolate and vanilla éclairs, sometimes round or horn-shaped, have most delicious cream fillings. Some places make a type of *apfelstrudel* which is sold hot, by the slice. You can also buy slices of *pizza* or little individual ones from a *pizzeria*; they are made from bread dough with all sorts of different fillings like anchovies, tuna, tomato, cheese, ham, herbs, olives, etc. The little buns that look like tea cakes are worth a try, though the raisins in them have pips. They are sometimes flavoured with cinnamon (*cannella*).

Cake mixes, made by Royal, can be bought but the cakes don't rise in the satisfactory English way. Self-raising flour is unobtainable but baking powder can be bought anywhere, either plain (*lievito*) or vanilla flavoured (*lievito vanigliato*). With no mixer and very often no mixing bowl, baking-tins or oven, cake making presents problems and is best abandoned. If cakes are an indispensable part of your diet, either bring them from home or come armed with cake mixes and baking tins (always supposing there is an oven), or buy them—though this is a sure way of using up holiday money.

Pasta

PASTA (short for *pastaciutta*, meaning dried paste or dough) comes in innumerable shapes and sizes and is sold all over Italy. Some of the names vary locally but the types fall into roughly four categories:

1. *Pasta* to put in soups
2. *Spaghetti*, noodles etc., usually served with a sauce
3. *Pasta* with a filling made of meat, herbs, vegetables or cheese, like *ravioli*
4. Fancy shapes for serving like *spaghetti*

We list below some of the types you are most likely to find in each category. It is either made from finely ground flour from the heart of the wheat grain (*pasta di pura semola di grano duro*), or with egg and flour (*all' uovo*) or with the addition of spinach (*verde*) which doesn't taste particularly spinachy but is an interesting green colour. The best is home-made (*fatta in casa*).

1. *capelli d'angele*   very fine threads of pasta like *vermicelli*
   maccheroncini   little pieces of macaroni
   pastine   general term for small shapes
   stellete   tiny star shapes
   semini   shapes like grains of Patna rice
   tagliolini
   tonnarelli   } very fine string egg pasta (can also be served with sauce like *spaghetti*)
   tonnellini
   vermicelli   very fine threads of *pasta*
2. *fettucine*   noodles from Rome
   fusilli   skeins of noodles
   lasagne   wide noodles
   lasagne verde   wide noodles made with spinach
   maccheroni   macaroni
   pappardelle   wide noodles
   rigatoni   large corrugated macaroni tubes

spaghetti	spaghetti (incidentally, never tinned)
spaghettini	very thick *spaghetti*
tagliatelle	noodles
tagliolini	
tonnarelli	very fine string egg pasta (can also be put in soup)
tonnellini	
trenette	long thin *pasta* from Genoa
3. *agnolotti*	small stuffed envelopes, like *ravioli*
anolini	small stuffed envelopes, like *ravioli*
cannelloni	large rolled up squares of *pasta* with meat and herb filling. Sold as hollow rolls, ready for filling at home
cappelletti	('little hats'), twists of stuffed *pasta*
manicotti	large tubes, like *cannelloni*
panzaretti	little envelopes, like *ravioli*
ravioli	can nearly always be bought freshly made, to be cooked at home in boiling water, then served with tomato sauce and grated parmesan. It makes one realise how unlike the real thing is tinned *ravioli*
tortellini	little rings of egg *pasta* with a delicate filling; can also be bought fresh to cook at home—especially good in Bologna
tortelloni	large coils of stuffed *pasta*, less delicate than tortellini
4. *chiocciole*	shells
conchiglie	shells
farfalle	butterflies
farfalloni	larger butterflies
orecchiette	ear-shaped *pasta*

POLENTA. Flour made from ground maize. Add to boiling salted water, stir and simmer it for about 20 minutes until it thickens like semolina. Cool it in a shallow dish and when it is cold it can be cut into squares, fried in oil like croquettes, and served with grated cheese or tomato sauce. (Approx. 1⅓ cups of polenta per 1 litre of water, although a coarser ground polenta may need more water.)

Miscellaneous Groceries

ASPIC JELLY is sold in most supermarkets.

BREAKFAST CEREALS. There is little choice, apart from Kelloggs Cornflakes, (made in Italy and called *fiocchi d'avena* reasonably priced) and Rice Krispies (expensive).

CHOCOLATE SPREAD. There is a nut-flavoured variety called *Nutella*, usually popular with children.

FLOUR. There is no self-raising flour, though baking powder and yeast (both called *lievito*) can be bought. Plain flour is sold everywhere.

GOLDEN SYRUP is not obtainable.

HONEY both thick and thin, is sold everywhere.

HORSE-RADISH SAUCE, called *cren*, is not creamy like ours but consists of finely grated horse radish floating in vinegar. It goes well with boiled chicken, beef and tongue.

JAM. Italian jams are excellent and really taste of fruit. If you like chestnuts you might try *marmellata di marroni*, a thick marron cream, delicious spread on a hunk of bread and butter. *Marmellata di amarene* is a bitter-sweet jam made from Morello cherries; the Italians serve it with ice cream which usually proves too sour for children, but should appeal to a more sophisticated palate. Imported English jams are very expensive.

JELLIES come in crystal form, in raspberry and strawberry flavours. They make up as well as ours but cost twice as much.

KETCHUP called *catchup* or *rubra* costs more than twice as much as English brands, but tastes the same.

MARMALADE is sold everywhere but called orange jam—*marmellata di arance*.

MARMITE is not obtainable. Nor is Bovril.

MAYONNAISE either plain or lemon flavoured, is perfectly delicious and tastes really home-made. There is no sharp-tasting salad cream.

MUSTARD. Italian-made 'Orco' is more like a French Mustard and very good. In tourist areas there are several imported brands, including Colman's mustard powder.

OIL. Olive oil is extremely dear. *Olio di semi*, made from sunflower seeds, is very reasonable, sold everywhere and equally good for cooking or salads.

PACKET SOUPS. There is a good range of these at reasonable prices. Many of them cater for Italian palates—*minestrone*, clear soups with *pasta*, and the Venetian speciality *risi e bisi*, a very thick soup of peas, ham and rice. The frozen fish soup-cum-stew (*zuppa di pesce*) is well worth a try.

PEPPER, black and white, is sold either in little plastic containers or loose, by the *etto* (100 grammes). The ground black pepper is rather coarse, like peppercorns ground through a mill. Peppercorns are also available everywhere.

RICE grown in Northern Italy, but available everywhere, is all of the round grain variety. It responds best to gentle cooking, should be rescued from the stove when still slightly nutty in the centre and not allowed to go mushy.

SALT can only be bought at tobacconists (tabaccheria).

SUGAR. Granulated and lump sugar is sold everywhere but not caster or brown sugar. Some exclusive delicatessens in large towns sell them very highly priced. Icing sugar is usually sold loose, by the *etto*.

VINEGAR. Small shops tend to stock only one make of wine vinegar (a pinkish colour) but in towns you can buy tarragon, red and white wine vinegar. It is all milder than malt vinegar.

Beverages and Soft Drinks

TEA. As we mentioned in the introduction, tea is very expensive. The tiniest packet (50 grammes) costs more than $\frac{1}{4}$ lb. in England, so for avid tea-drinkers it's worth taking out as much tea as possible. Tea-bags are comparatively less expensive and come in minimum packets of twenty. All the tea is Indian.

COFFEE. Italian coffee is first-class and inexpensive, well worth the slight trouble of making it. Instant coffee is very expensive and the de-caffeinated variety a third of the price more. Coffee and de-caffeinated coffee can both be bought ground or unground. Freeze-dried coffee, Gran Aroma (like Gold Blend) is available but very dear.

COCOA. There are two types of cocoa powder, sweetened and bitter, the bitter being more expensive. There are a number of malted bedtime drinks.

MILKSHAKE MIXES are available in powdered form and in various flavours.

MINERAL WATER. There are many brands at varying prices and they can be bought at the grocer, wine shop or chemist. There is a small deposit charged on the bottle, refundable on return. A lot of people drink mineral water abroad in preference to tap water but, for those who cannot bear the fizzy, Epsom salty taste, tap water is perfectly drinkable in all but the most primitive places. Camping sites lay on drinking water (*acqua potabile*) but it might be wise to stick to mineral water in the extreme south when water is scarce. There is a non-fizzy brand for children called San Gemini.

FRUIT DRINKS. There are no fruit squashes to be diluted with water. The nearest equivalent is a fruit syrup (*sciroppo*) which is very sticky and sweet and is drunk diluted with mineral water by Italian children. The flavours include strawberry, raspberry and mint.

However, there are plenty of bottled fruit drinks and the ubiquitous Coca-Cola. Most of the bottled drinks are fizzy and include flavours like orange, lemon and ginger. The nearest equivalent in flavour to diluted orange squash is 'Sol D'Oro' which is sold by the carton in supermarkets. One carton is enough for one glass and it is far cheaper than the little bottles, but then the juice is less concentrated.

There is a good range of sweetened fruit juices including orange, pear, apple, apricot and tomato. These are delicious and really taste of natural fruit but, as with all these bottled drinks, they're an expensive way of quenching your thirst.

Non-alcoholic aperitifs like Campari, Cinzano and Martini are cheap and taste just like their alcoholic counterparts. Served ice-cold they are a refreshing mid-day drink and don't have the same soporific effect, combined with sun, as wine and spirits do. Look for 'analcoolico' on the label. Tonic water, ginger ale and soda water (not in syphons) can be bought, but not bitter lemon.

Wine

Italy produces more wine than any other country in Europe, though the acreage of vineyards is less than in France. We are apt to think that Chianti is the only wine that comes from Italy, but in fact there are numerous other varieties, many of them delicious. Chianti is in fact produced in only a small area south of Florence, so half the wine one sees in straw-covered flasks is probably local hooch disguised to look like Chianti.

Each district produces several different wines and it is much better to drink the local wine, bottled on the spot, since the best of the vintage is always kept there and it will be cheaper too. The less good quality is sent off in casks to other parts of the country where it is bottled and sometimes mixed with other wines. The safest plan is to drink wine from another area only if it's been bottled where it was grown. This should be stated on the label.

Since 1963 a new wine law has been introduced to ensure that each regional wine has been made by the right method, with the right grapes and in the right district. The neck labels are numbered for each wine grower so that he fills a guaranteed number of bottles and no more. The law states that bottles with a capacity of up to 5 litres, marked *controllata* or *controllata e guarantita*, must show on the label the denomination of origin, the amount of wine in the bottle, the name and locality of the wine producer and of the firm which bottles it. Although the officials responsible for implementing these measures may vary in strictness and efficiency, the overall standard of wine has improved. There is considerably less 'sophisticated' wine around and chaptalisation (adding sugar to wine) is forbidden.

It is sold in supermarkets, wine merchants' (*vine e liquori*) and most grocers'.

The local wines may vary in quality but it is worth experimenting till you find one you like. You can always ask a waiter in a bar or café what he would recommend; he is less likely to suggest the most expensive, unlike a wine waiter or wine merchant.

There are several very sweet wines around, in red, white and rosé, so if you prefer a dry one, make sure it's *secco* and not *dolce*. Any red wine less than *grado* 12° or white less than *grado* 11° is highly doubtful. The degrees of alcohol should be marked on the label.

Nearly every region in Italy produces wine; the north and central part produce finer wines than the south, where much of it is coarse and used for blending (Campania, Calabria and Basilicata in particular make a lot of blending wine). The following regions all produce wine, and as long as one isn't tempted into making comparisons with good burgundies and clarets, the search for a pleasant wine should be far from disappointing.

Abruzzi and Molise
Apulia and Calabria
Campania,
   including Capri and Ischia
Elba
Emilia-Romagna
Friuli-Venezia Giulia
Liguria
Lombardy
Lazio
Le Marche
Piedmont
Sardinia
Sicily
Trentino-Alto-Adige
Tuscany
Umbria
Veneto

SPARKLING WINES. Asti Spumante and Moscata d'Asti are sweet sparkling wines. Wines labelled as Gran Spumante or similar are liable to be dry and more expensive. Only one can be described as champagne (made by Martini by the *Méthode Champenoise*); French champagne can be found, though it is by no means cheap.

BRANDY. Italian brandy is cheap and very drinkable though not particularly good. French and Spanish can also be bought, though these are more expensive.

GRAPPA like the French *marc*, is made from grape pressings and varies from an abrasive fire-water to an enjoyable *digestif*. The cheaper makes are best avoided.

LIQUEURS. Many of the liqueurs are the same as the French ones —*crème de menthe, crème de cacao*, cherry brandy etc.—though some may have a different name e.g. Certosa for Chartreuse. They often come in a most ingenious array of bottles (some in miniatures too) and cost mostly under one pound. Some of them can be very sickly sweet; one often finds that the more gimmicky the bottle, the less palatable the contents.

VERMOUTHS AND APERITIFS. Italian aperitifs are legion. Some are made from the most unlikely things like rhubarb (*Rabarbaro*) or cardoons[1] (Cynar). A large number have a distinct flavour of cough mixture, many of them are very sweet and are more palatable diluted with soda water. Some, like Elixir di China and Ramazzotti, are drunk hot. Carpano Punt e Mes, Bitter Cinzano, Campari Soda or Dry Martini (which in a bar won't automatically be served with gin unless you ask for it) are pleasant for anyone who likes a dry aperitif. Several are sold in small bottles, enough for one glass, so you can always experiment economically instead of lashing out on a bottle of something you find you don't like, though in fact the prices are about half what they are in England. Contrary to general belief, vermouth gradually deteriorates once the bottle has been opened.

BEER is all of the light, continental type. Quite a lot is imported from Switzerland but this costs nearly twice as much as Italian beer.

WHISKY. Several brands are available, all imported and, surprisingly, cheaper than they are in England.

[1] Similar to a globe artichoke.

GIN. Italian-made gin is cheaper, less dry and lower proof than ours, but one can buy imported makes of British gin at higher prices.

SPAIN

General

Because of the poor grazing and lack of arable land, meat and dairy products are expensive. Fruit, vegetables and bread are cheap. Fish varies enormously from one area to another, as indeed do all prices between a tourist resort and a small village; in some places one can pay three to four times as much as in others. Supermarkets tend to be very expensive, but one is paying for convenience and a higher standard of hygiene. Grocers' shops which have a monopoly of trade in a small area will put their prices up.

The cheapest place is the municipal market, a series of lock-up stalls, some owned by shop-keepers, others by the growers themselves. They are to be found in most small and all large towns and sell fruit, vegetables, meat, poultry, fish, cheese, cooked meats of the *salami* type and some groceries. At their worst they can be fly-blown and knee-deep in paper, orange peel and squashed water-melons; they won't put fruit in paper bags, so be well prepared with a sturdy shopping basket into which potatoes, tomatoes and peaches may cascade—preferably in that order! The more enlightened markets put everything into polythene bags, have better refrigeration facilities and have an information office where you can have things re-weighed or make complaints if you're not satisfied. These small markets are a marvellous way to see Spanish life in the raw and, although it will take far longer than whisking round a supermarket, it will certainly save your precious holiday pesetas.

Tinned food is very expensive, but there is a good range of reasonably priced frozen vegetables, some fish and one or two traditional Spanish dishes like *Paella* and *Bacalao a la Vizcaína* —a good way of trying them out and cheaper than a restaurant.

Some restaurants do a *paella* to take away, which again works out cheaper than eating out. You order it ahead and collect it, piping hot, in the *paella* pan at the appointed hour. It can be kept hot on top of the stove but is better eaten immediately. If the restaurant is nearby, they may deliver the *paella*—but establish this as a certainty. We once sat waiting for an hour, berating the dilatory Spanish, only to find that they were waiting for us to fetch it!

In small villages the shops are well-hidden, and it is often only by peering through open doorways and seeing a pile of melons or sacks of rice and sugar that you know you've discovered one. But the trend is for shopkeepers to be less reticent and the following names outside shops will give you some idea of what they sell—we say 'some idea' because the demarcation tends to be confusingly fluid. Whether these are self-imposed restrictions or local legislation is anybody's guess, but we have known bread shops that sell every type of alcohol and soft drink, but not beer on Sundays, and milk, never; grocers' shops that sell every type of sliced, wrapped loaf but no freshly baked bread; delicatessens where they will make you fresh sandwiches of ham, sausage, etc., but can't sell the bread on its own.

baker's	*panadería*
butcher's	*carnicería*
cake shop	*pastelería, confitería*
cooked meats (delicatessen)	*salchichonería, jamonería*
fishmonger's	*pescadería*
greengrocer's	*frutas y verduras*
grocer's	*ultramarinos, comestibles*
	alimentación
poulterer's	*pollería*

The shopping hours are generally 9 a.m.—2.0 p.m. and 5.0 p.m.—8.30 or 9.0 p.m. The smaller shops often work longer hours in the season and will open for part of Sunday morning, though since this is now illegal, they frequently have a furtive air about them, with the blinds still down and customers hurriedly nipping inside.

Far more confusing are the innumerable national holidays and Saints' days that crop up without any warning; all shops and banks shut everywhere and one can really be caught on the hop with no money or food. Below is a list of the principal holidays in Spain but it doesn't include local *fiestas*. These are usually well advertised and can go on for as long as a week, so find out from your local shops, travel agents or *Ayuntamiento* (town hall) on which days everywhere stays closed.

New Year's Day	29th June
6th January	18th July
19th March	25th July
Maundy Thursday (afternoon)	
Good Friday	15th August
Easter Sunday	12th October
1st May	1st November
Ascension Day	8th December
Corpus Christi	25th December

The equipment provided in Spanish kitchens is very often inadequate. Kettles, teapots and strainers are rare, egg whisks, mincers and garlic crushers rarer. (This last may not be essential, but it's easier than wrestling with a pestle and mortar, the normal substitute.) Cooking pans are limited to a couple of vast cauldrons in which you could merrily cook spaghetti for twenty people, (if only they weren't so thick that it takes nearly a gas cylinder to boil the water), a small saucepan, a *paella* pan (large shallow pan with two loop handles), a frying pan and sometimes a ridged frying pan : these are used for frying steak and fish if there is no grill, since the ridges produce lines on the steak and fish to look as if they'd been charcoal-grilled.

Ovens often can't be regulated; they just go on getting hotter.

Fish

There is a good variety of Mediterranean and Atlantic fish and shellfish, but it is surprisingly expensive unless you can buy it straight off the fishing boats. Much of the fish caught in the Atlantic is frozen, sent to Madrid and then distributed to fishmongers. Some deal exclusively in frozen fish—*congelados*.

The best fresh fish is to be found in municipal markets, where the turnover is more rapid. The prices vary from one stall to another and are written up on slates. They are not easy to decipher because half are written in dialect and the other half are so badly spelt that they bear no resemblance to dictionary Spanish! If you ask the stallholder to identify them, ten to one his accent is so thick that you are still none the wiser. However, there is a list opposite which gives the varieties you are most likely to meet.

Many of the fish are large with alarmingly ugly heads, which are unfortunately included in the weight when paid for. The fishmonger will clean them if you ask (*'Se puede limpiarlo?'*) and will present you with the head, etc., to make stock, unless you don't want it. (*'Me quite la cabeza, por favor'*). The really cheap and plentiful fish are the fresh sardines and anchovies, which are excellent value and delicious, and some of the bigger fish like swordfish, tunny, sea-bream and red mullet are well worth a try. Recipes are given on pp. 120-127. If you like the flavour of lobster, you might try angler fish (*rape*) which is said to taste of lobster—in fact some restaurants are not above filling lobster shells with it and passing them off as the real thing.

Pre-packed frozen fish, either filleted or cut into slices, is beginning to be more widely sold. Some of it appears in rather amateurish-looking polythene packets with just the name and no picture to go by, so unless you understand Spanish you don't know what you are getting. There are some excellent frozen croquettes which come in a variety of flavours (shrimp, hake, cheese). They contain quite a lot of potato but are quick and easy to fry and popular with children.

Tinned sardines, anchovies and tuna abound, and since they are home-produced, they are reasonably priced. There is also a good choice of tinned shellfish including mussels, cockles, squid and shrimps, sometimes in a spicy sauce (*en escabeche*). Vacuum-packed smoked swordfish is delicious as an hors d'oeuvre. Here is a list of some of the fish and shellfish:

alacha	large sardines	*carpon*	gurnard,
almejas	cockles		gurnet
almejones	scallops	*cazón*	dogfish
alosa	shad	*chirlas*	clams
anchoas	anchovies	*conchas de*	
anguila	eel	*San Jaime*	scallops
arana	weever	*conchas*	
arenque	herring	*peregrinas*	scallops
atún	tuna, tunny fish	*cóngrio*	conger eel
		chopa	sea bream
		cigala	Dublin bay
bacalao	dried salt cod		prawn
besugo	sea-bream gilt-head		
		dorada	gilt-head, sea-
baila	sea trout		bream
boga	bream family		
bogabante	lobster	*emperador*	swordfish
bogavante	lobster	*espadín*	sprat
bonito	tuna, tunny fish	*estornino*	Spanish mackerel
boquerón	anchovy	*esturión*	sturgeon
breca	sea-bream		
		gallina del	gurnard,
caballa	mackerel	*mar*	gurnet
calamares	squid, cuttlefish	*gallo*	John Dory (Andalusia)
camarones			
cangrejos de mar	shrimps sea crabs	*gambas*	prawns
cangrejos de río	river crabs	*lamprea*	lamprey
		langosta	lobster
carpa	carp	*langostina*	crayfish

lenguado	sole	*rape*	angler fish
lisa	grey mullet		frogfish
lobo marino	sea-bass	*rascacio*	rascasse
lubina	sea-bass	*raspallón*	grey-bream
lucio	pike	*raya*	skate
		rodaballo	turbot
mejillones	mussels	*rubio*	red gurnard
merluza	hake		
mugle	grey mullet	*sabala*	shad
mujiol	grey mullet	*salmonete*	red mullet
		sardina	sardines
ostras	oysters	*sargo*	grey bream
		saupa	sea-bream
pagel	Spanish bream		family
pargo	red sea-bream		
perca	perch	*trucha*	trout
pescadilla	whiting		
pez espada	swordfish	*verdel*	mackerel
platija	plaice		
		zafio	conger eel

Meat

Meat can be bought either in a *carnicería*, in some supermarkets or in the municipal market. There are two sources of meat: fresh and imported frozen. The fresh meat is very expensive, almost double the price of the frozen, and because of the climate it is sold as soon as it is slaughtered instead of being hung first, so it can be tough.

The meat is divided into three or four price categories, according to the quality, not necessarily the cut. The price of all home-reared meat varies by a few pesetas but by law the price lists must be displayed for the customer to see. If you can find either a French-Algerian butcher or one mostly patronised by French customers, the meat will be of a higher standard.

BEEF AND VEAL. The most expensive category is the leanest and includes steaks and escalopes, but equally stewing steak and mince. You just point to the bit you like the look of and the butcher will ask you whether you'd like it in fillets or chopped up. He will then hack away, regardless of the grain. Sometimes the best steaks are upgraded into a category called *extra*. In smaller places, mince is done to order and is not on view. Just choose your piece of meat and they will mince it for you.

The second category has much more gristle and fat and is twenty or twenty-five pence a kilo cheaper. English people who live in Spain tend to use it for dog meat, so the third category is best left well alone! The beef and veal is all called *ternera* and half the time it is anybody's guess as to which it is. Even the butchers seem unable to distinguish between them and where one will cut you an escalope from a piece of meat, his mate will gaily slice a steak for the next customer from the same piece. It is much more like *vitellone* in Italy (see p. 54); really young veal is called *lechera* and is very difficult to find.

Some enlightened butchers make fresh hamburgers on the spot; the addition of garlic and fresh parsley, and the subtraction of preservatives, make them very tasty.

escalope	*escalope*
fillet steak (and other steaks)	*filete*
mince	*carne picada*
rib	not sold as a joint; they cut the meat out and sell the bones for soup
sirloin	*solomillo*
stewing steak	*carne para guisar*
beef and veal	ternera

LAMB. The expensive category includes chops and leg, the second price is for shoulder and the third little more than scraps for stewing. Stewing lamb can also be cut from the leg and the bones bashed to splinters; unless you are prepared to dictate your needs, they will literally butcher it. It is possible to buy a whole leg for roasting. Though expensive, the lamb is good on the whole, but scraggy—not surprisingly, since one sees sheep grazing among the rocks with no blade of grass in sight.

breast	*pecho de cordero*
chop and cutlet	*chuleta*
lamb	*cordero*
leg	*pierna de cordero*
shoulder	*espalda*
sucking lamb	*lechón* (Northern Spain)

PORK. This again is expensive compared with England. The first category includes loin chops and any lean meat; the second ribs and the third knuckle, pigs' trotters and salt pork.

Pork butchers make their own sausages; red ones, black ones and English-looking pink ones. These last are very good fried, once you have unwound the string with which they are festooned. Though slightly saltier than ours, they contain less preservative. There are no skinless, frozen or beef sausages.

There are various salami types of sausage, including one fierce-looking orangey-red one that looks as if it has bathed in ketchup; called *sobresada*, it comes from Mallorca, is surprisingly mild and very good.

Chorizo is coarser and there are two types, one used cold in slices for an *hors d'oeuvres* and the other cooked in chunks in stews like the traditional *fabada asturiano*. This is made with dried haricot beans, tomato sauce, garlic, salt pork and various bits of sausage and is the Spanish equivalent of the French *cassoulet*. (The *fabada* is sold in tins if you'd like to try some.)

Morcilla asturiana is a kind of black pudding.

BACON is expensive and rather salty. In small shops it is sliced off unhealthily dark-looking joints but tastes far better than it looks. Supermarkets and grocers in more tourist-conscious areas stock pre-packed rashers, paper thin and very good. Pork butchers keep two sorts: *tocino graso* is the very fatty bacon cut in small pieces and used either in stews or for larding joints. *Tocino magro* makes a reasonable substitute for cold boiled bacon.

Cooked ham is imported from Poland in large tins but sold in slices in the normal way. One can also buy it in small tins, though it is more like corned beef than ham.

PORK

fillet	*filete*
leg	*pierna*
loin	*lomo de cerdo*
loin chop	*chuleta de lomo*
pork	*cerdo*
Pork Products	
bacon (frying)	*bacón*
bacon (boiling)	*tocino magro*
bacon (fat or lardoons)	*tocino graso*
brawn	*cabeza de Jabali*
ham (cooked)	*jamón de York*
ham (raw, like Parma)	*jamón serrano*
pressed pork	*jamón de Paris*
salami sausage	*salchichón*
sausages (frying)	*salchichas*

POULTRY. The chickens, despite their emaciated appearance, have plenty of flavour. The head and feet are included in the weight and though the butcher will cut these off and draw the giblets, he will graciously present you with them all in the same parcel. Frozen chickens are also sold but even the largest only weigh about 2½ lbs. However, you are spared the head and feet.

RABBIT. This is much more expensive than chicken, but very good.

chicken	*pollo, gallina*
duck	*pato*
rabbit	*conejo*

OFFAL. Liver (lambs, calves or pigs) is all the same price. Kidney is nearly all veal kidney and sold without suet. Both are reasonable. Sweetbreads are generally sold attached to lights and are hardly used in Spanish cooking.

FROZEN MEAT. This is imported from the Argentine and, occasionally, Poland. It is far more reliably tender and, being about half the price of fresh meat, is a much better buy. It is sold already defrosted by butchers who specialise in frozen meat, *carne congelada.* It is categorised in the same way as fresh meat but the prices, laid down by the Ministry of Commerce, are fixed.

TINNED MEATS. These are all very expensive and though there are a few exotic delicacies like stewed partridge, it would be much wiser to take tins out with you if you need them as a stand-by.

Dairy Produce

MILK. This is all sterilised, except in the north where it is possible to buy fresh milk. The sterilised (homogenised, vitaminised and pasteurised) milk is sold in litre bottles with metal crown tops. It is not delivered and can be bought from the grocer, supermarket, *mantecaría* (literally, butter shop) and some bakers'. A deposit is charged on all bottles, refunded on return of the empties. There are a number of different makes of milk and shops don't like taking back the empties of makes they don't stock. Milk is now being sold in half-litre cartons; it tastes better and is much easier to carry, though fitting the lop-sided pyramid shapes into the fridge requires enormous ingenuity.

Evaporated, condensed and powdered milk can all be bought.

In some areas it is possible to buy fresh goats' milk, but this should always be brought up to the boil three times before using, in case of Malta fever.

BUTTER. Most of the butter is unsalted but, if you prefer salted, ask for *mantequilla salada*. It is all home-produced and expensive.

EGGS are free range only in country areas and sold by the dozen or singly. They all seem small, although in the markets they are graded into three or four different sizes. Some tourist areas now sell them in cardboard or plastic cartons, but they are just as likely to hand them to you in a paper cornet or polythene bag, so the mortality rate is pretty high.

CREAM is not used much in Spanish cooking, so is only stocked in tourist areas or near the French border. It is likely to be fresher if bought in the municipal market. You have to take your own container, unless you are feeling reckless and rich enough to buy a litre bottle.

CHEESE. Because of poor grazing, there is not a great variety of cheese. The chief type is *Manchego*—some shopkeepers will tell you blithely that every cheese they stock is *Manchego*. It falls into two categories: *seco*—dry (crumbly, rather like Caerphilly) and *mantecoso*—buttery (bland, more like a Dutch cheese). It is all mild. Some of it comes in circular shapes, with either yellow or blackish rind, and some in oblongs with a red rind.

There is a round, red-covered cheese called Bola, similar to Edam.

Pena Santa, or Spanish Roquefort, is excellent, and is the only blue-veined cheese made in Spain. In tourist-conscious areas, you can buy Camembert, Brie, Danish Blue, grated Parmesan, Boursin, Gruyère and a pre-packed cheese proudly described as 'Austrian Alps Swiss Cheese aged over 100 days'! Tinned Brie and Camembert are very good. There is also a Spanish Brie, made under licence at Escorial, which is a good and cheap substitute for the real thing.

Cream cheese, freshly made from goats' milk, can be found in some markets. It appears in a white, pudding-basin shaped mound, and tastes like a mild cottage cheese. It will keep well in a fridge.

Processed cheese appears in a number of makes, Spanish and French. Laughing Cow (La Vaca que Ríe) and La Casería are both excellent. They do not make packets flavoured with tomato, shrimp, celery, etc.

MARGARINE. This is very much cheaper than butter and much more widely used by the Spanish for sandwiches. It is sometimes sold in cartons.

LARD. Called *manteca de cerdo*, lard comes in long sausage-shapes like salami, off which the required weight is cut. It is also to be seen at the butcher's in saucepans in which it has been rendered down.

OIL. The Spanish usually cook in olive oil which presents no storage problems in hot weather, but if you hate the smell it is possible to buy corn, groundnut and soya oil. In any case, don't go for the cheapest olive oil which can be very nasty. The only safe inexpensive ones are the supermarkets' own brands and Andres Ybarra.

YOGHOURT. This is sold either in cartons or jars. The jars carry a refundable deposit, are cheaper and contain more yoghourt, but only in natural or strawberry flavours. The cartons include apple, apricot, pear, pineapple and strawberry and are sweeter than the English ones. Danone make a variety called 'Supremo' in chocolate and caramel, more like the cream desserts now sold in England.

Vegetables and Fruit

The best time of year for vegetables is the spring and early summer, when there is a large and cheap variety of fresh produce —peas, broad beans, French beans, carrots, cabbage, chard, leeks, lettuce and, of course, tomatoes (which are available all the year round, becoming steadily more vast as the season progresses). In the summer it is wise to buy them on the green side; you will find they ripen very quickly and keep their delicious home-grown flavour.

From midsummer onwards cucumbers, courgettes, marrows, peppers and aubergines become more plentiful and lettuces more wilted. These are nearly always of the cos or density type; the inner leaves will generally respond to a quick dip in water, followed by a rest in a sealed plastic container or polythene bag in the fridge, from which they will emerge crisp a couple of hours later.

All vegetables are sold by weight, but nobody minds if you ask for three carrots or half a cabbage. Some stallholders need firm handling and you must be quite adamant if you only want one cucumber (even though they are rather small) or Manuel will try to fling in a couple more to make the weight up to a kilo. In southern Spain there are two potato crops a year, but if you want a rest from peeling and gouging out eyes (which abound), Knorr do a very good instant mashed potato.

Dried herbs are sold in markets, mostly for medicinal purposes; they aren't used much in Spanish cooking, but a few supermarkets are starting to stock them. Fresh parsley looks rather like wilting maidenhair fern but is perfectly all right for cooking, though useless as a garnish. Sage and bay leaves can occasionally be tracked down, but if you like to use herbs a lot it would be better to take dried ones out with you. We have found delicious thyme and rosemary growing wild in the country.

The following vegetables may need a few words of explanation.

SALAD ONIONS. There are no slim spring onions but the special large mild variety (*cebollos verdes*) are round, and quite delicious.

RADISHES are more the size of carrots and look most un-radish like. They are mild and not very juicy.

FRENCH BEANS. As well as the thin tubular kind a few inches long, there is a sort that looks more like a flattened pea pod with tiny peas in. It needs no stringing, is very tender and appears in July.

CUCUMBERS are often so short they look more like courgettes.

TOMATOES. Many of them are vast and look distinctly unripe but even the palest orange ones are full of juice and really taste of tomato. Excellent for salads but not for frying. However, they ripen quickly in hot weather (so do peppers) and may change from green to red in a day or two.

Aubergines, courgettes, peppers, artichokes and chard are similar to those found in Italy and a description is found on pp. 62, 63, 64.

FROZEN VEGETABLES are cheap and very good. In addition to the usual peas, beans and mixed veg. (which include artichoke hearts), there are brussels sprouts, cauliflower, spinach and artichokes.

TINNED VEGETABLES are expensive, except for tomatoes and pimentos. There are various permutations of the tomato, onion, aubergine, courgette and pimento mixture, sometimes as a salad or sauce, and all very good. Look out for *Chanfaina* or *Sanfaina*, the Spanish equivalent of *ratatouille*; and *Pisto Manchego*, a very good tomato sauce. Both these make delicious additions to fish, meat and chicken casseroles. Prices vary enormously and it is worth shopping around if you want to stock up your store cupboard. Some of the cheaper tins look suspiciously bashed and rusty but we have so far suffered no ill effects from them.

Fresh mushrooms tend to be elusive; they need peeling and

are rather sandy. There are several brands of tinned mushrooms.

FRUIT. Fresh fruit in season is plentiful and cheap. Next to nothing is imported since Spain and the Canaries between them grow just about everything. Easter and early summer bring cherries and small, sweet strawberries; July and August produce yellow and red plums, yellow and white peaches and, from mid-August on, melon, water melon, prickly pear and custard apples. Oranges, lemons, apples and bananas are available all the year round—the latter arrive from the Canaries still attached to part of the tree and are hacked from the branch when you buy them—most satisfying!

FIGS (*higos*). After the familiar brown dried figs we see at home, it may be a surprise to find the fresh ones are a purpley blue when ripe (green when unripe). Once they are over-ripe they split and bruise easily, so eat them as soon as they're just right. They are perfectly delicious and don't taste of syrup of figs.

CUSTARD APPLES (*chirimoyas*), found chiefly in southern Spain, look like smooth-sided globe artichokes with the spikes ironed out. You don't eat the skin or the fat, black pips, but the rest of the fruit is juicy (or rather creamy) like a ripe avocado pear or a rare and delicate mousse. The flavour is delicious, sweet and mild. Eat them soon after buying, because they bruise and ripen rapidly. The children found them easiest to tackle cut in half and eaten with a teaspoon.

PRICKLY PEAR (*higo chumbo*) is best approached with a pair of wicket keeper's gloves to protect you from the myriad minute prickles which will embed themselves instantly into your flesh. Not content with that, they become totally invisible and you may itch all over without being able to find them. However, if you are not daunted by the prospect of such physical discomfort, at least make sure that you go to the market armed with a solid shopping basket and not a string bag. The prickly pear is about the size of a duck egg, a faintly blushing green with neatly dotted clusters of spines. Inside it is very juicy, refreshing and sweet, but full of pips.

POMEGRANATES are also full of pips and juice, if you don't mind negotiating the former to enjoy the latter. They sometimes appear in English shops, so their shiny, orangey-red, onion shape may already be a familiar sight.

QUINCE look like small green pears. They take ages to cook but if you have a pressure cooker or unlimited gas they are a delicious substitute for stewed apple. They have a slightly gritty texture and need plenty of sugar. As with apple, the flavour can be enhanced by the addition of honey and a couple of cloves.

PEACHES. The luscious yellow variety needs no description. You may also come across some smaller peaches, which look squashed and mis-shapen; these are not rejects but *paraguayas*. They are very good and well worth trying, despite their distressing tendency to secrete the odd maggot around their stones.

LEMONS may look green and bulging; they are not unripe but are cheap and excellent.

Bread, Cakes and Biscuits

BREAD. Spanish bread has improved enormously over the last year or two. The French type of loaf, which is very cheap, is best bought each day but, if this is impossible, keep it wrapped in polythene and/or warm it up in the oven next day. Wholemeal bread (*pan integral*) stays fresh longer.

Wrapped, sliced loaves of brown (*pan negro* or *pan moreno*) and white bread can be bought. Produced by Bimbo of Barcelona, they are a distinct improvement on English mass-produced bread and are useful for sandwiches and fried bread. Bimbo also do a limited range of snack rolls, buns and cakes, all conveniently pre-packed and fresh.

The equivalents of French *biscottes*, a cross between a rusk and melba toast, is called *biscotel*. It comes in various shapes and sizes, salted or unsalted. The children love them for breakfast instead of toast, and they are very good with cheese. There is no Spanish-made crispbread. Some bakers make *croissants*.

CAKES. Spanish *pâtisserie* can be very deceiving; it looks good but can be dry as sawdust or terribly sweet and sickly. Cakes for cutting into slices are rare. True, there is a madeira type of cake with a little fruit in it called, misleadingly, 'plum cake' (which in fact the Spanish eat for breakfast) but if you crave a Victoria sponge, take cake mixes and baking tins with you. Even this may be a risky substitute since Spanish ovens are notoriously capricious.

There are no jam or treacle tarts or fruit pies; if these are an indispensable part of your diet, go armed with golden syrup and pastry mixes. Experience has proved that making pastry with Spanish flour, lard or margarine and rolling it out with a milk bottle is a chore and a failure.

BISCUITS. Biscuits, sweet and savoury, abound. The savoury sorts, like crackers and cheese-flavoured biscuits, are very good; so are the semi-sweet like digestive and Marie. But among sweet biscuits, snares and delusions are legion; they can be sawdusty, tasteless or synthetically sickly. The more expensive ones are a safer bet but, if the packet doesn't list butter, *manteca, mantequilla*, among the ingredients, you could be in real trouble! They are all marginally dearer than in Britain and the variety is limited to filled wafers, chocolate-covered and plain sweet biscuits—no custard creams, bourbon, ginger or iced biscuits.

You may come across the following specialities, both savoury and sweet, which we found delicious:

Coca. A flan sold by the slice, hot or cold, made with onions, tuna fish, olives and tomato, rather like a *pizza.*

Individual pies, containing red pimento, tuna and onion.

A cake shaped like a French loaf and filled with pumpkin jam. This filling, romantically called 'angel's hair' (*cabello de angel*), is used in various regional pastries.

Churros are made from batter which is piped through a forcing bag into boiling oil, crisply fried then sprinkled with sugar. Traditionally they are eaten for breakfast and are perfectly delicious—even better if freshly made, so if you come across a *churro* stall at a fiesta, fair or market, do try them. The loops are sometimes threaded onto dried grass—most picturesque!

Turrón is Spanish nougat, not only the hard sort with nuts in it, but several variations on the egg, sugar and almond theme: a *fondant* of ground almonds with or without candied fruit, a soft but crunchy nougat with chopped almonds and *tortas imperiales*, sold in tins, which are more like small, thin biscuits. Much of it is made in Alicante or at nearby Jijona; you can look round some of the factories there and taste it.

Miscellaneous Groceries

ASPIC JELLY (*gelatina aspic*) is sold in crystal form in packets; it is very good, useful for a cold meal. You can put in it mixtures of things like ham, cooked chicken, shellfish, hard boiled eggs, tomatoes, cucumber, peas, even blobs of *pâté* or cream cheese. If you have no fridge and the weather is hot, make the jelly up with less water than given on the packet. Half water, half white wine (a light dry one) is particularly good with chicken or fish.

BABY FOODS. There are several variations of strained babyfoods available in jars, but not the coarser Junior foods. Packets of cereals for mixing with milk can be bought, but they are not cheap (nor, incidentally, are disposable nappies).

CEREALS. The two home-produced breakfast cereals are *Mait* (cornflakes) and *Crisp* (rice crispies). They are marginally less sweet and crisp than English varieties but a perfectly adequate substitute. If your palate demands something less plebeian, you'd better take it with you. Incidentally, individual packets are invaluable for travelling.

CHOCOLATE SPREAD has just appeared on the market, with and without chopped hazelnuts.

CORNFLOUR can be bought anywhere. It is mostly marketed under the brand-name 'Maizena'.

CRISPS come in polythene packets. They are very good, ready salted, with a faint aura of cooking oil. So far, no different flavours. They are called *Chips*.

CURRY POWDER and curry sauce can be bought in any tourist area but they are not cheap. Cold chicken curry served with rice, tomato salad, green salad and sliced banana makes a refreshing lunch on a hot day.

FLOUR (*harina*) is only plain, not self-raising, and is sold in maddening polythene bags that are difficult to open without spilling.

GELATINE is not obtainable.

GOLDEN SYRUP can occasionally be bought in tourist areas.

HONEY (*miel*). This is home-produced, gorgeous and very runny. It is often sold in containers that can be used as glasses afterwards. There is no thick honey.

JAM (*mermelada*). There are plenty of varieties of jam, mostly sold in tins. They tend to be rather runny and sweet and include strawberry, peach and greengage (this last is very good). Jars are more expensive, but on the other hand tinned jam needs decanting into a jar with a lid (to ward off wasps), unless you are lucky enough to possess a jam pot.

JELLIES (*gelatinas*). There is a limited range of jellies. They are sold in crystal form in packets and have rather synthetic flavours. These include strawberry, raspberry and orange. They are greatly improved by a squeeze of fresh orange or lemon juice when making them up. The addition of fresh or tinned fruit helps the taste too. If the weather is hot and you have no fridge, make them up with less liquid than given on the packet.

KETCHUP (*catsup*) made by Vida is available everywhere.

MARMALADE (*mermelada de naranja*), like jam, is sweet, runny and sold in tins. If you prefer it more chunky and bitter, ask for it, *amarga*; there is one brand that describes itself '*amarga*— English taste' and is excellent. Despite the acres of lemon trees, only orange marmalade is made.

MARMITE is rarely obtainable; some tourist areas stock Bovril.

MAYONNAISE (*mayonesa*). There are some excellent brands of mayonnaise. On the whole the more expensive ones are better and taste really home-made. None of them has the sharp taste of English salad cream.

MUSTARD (*mostaza*) is ready mixed and all of the French type, in varying strengths. It is very good but if you prefer English mustard, take your own.

NUTS. There are some lovely home-produced salted almonds (*almendras*) but apart from that, not much choice.

OLIVES (*aceitunas*), black, green, large, small, stuffed with pimento, almonds or anchovies (especially good), can be bought anywhere. You can either get them in tins (the larger, the cheaper, and the olives will keep provided they are covered in their brine) or you can buy them loose from the market or grocer's, where they will be scooped out of enormous barrels or tins, weighed and presented to you in the inevitable polythene bag. Some people never acquire the taste for olives, but we do urge anyone hesitating, to try the anchovy-stuffed ones.

PASTA (for description and uses see Italian section, pp. 68-69). There is a good selection of pasta for soups and plenty of *spaghetti*, macaroni and noodles, all cheap, but no fresh *tortellini* or *ravioli*. Tinned *spaghetti* is not cheap.

PÂTÉ. The inexpensive brands are good for biscuit-spreads.

PEPPER (*pimienta*), black and white, is sold ready ground. Peppercorns and red pepper (*pimientón*) can also be bought.

PUDDINGS. There are no cold pudding mixes and we usually go armed with instant whips for the children. A few blancmange mixes can be found but the most ubiquitous is misleadingly called 'Flan' (or 'Flanin') and is in fact a *crème caramel* (found on every Spanish menu). Of the two ready-made sweets, *membrillo* is well worth a try. It is made of quince and sold in slabs looking like carbolic soap. It is rich, sweet and slightly gritty, but delicious, especially if chilled.

The other, called *dulce holandés*, is sold in round plastic containers, divided into three sections, one flavour in each—chocolate, plain and pink; we say 'pink' because it's impossible to tell what it's meant to be. Our family greeted it with horror and summed it up as a cross between 'Play Doh' and soap. It is, however, a great favourite with Spanish children.

RICE (*arroz*) is all home grown and round grain. It goes mushy if overcooked; it is ready when very slightly nutty in the centre, and needs to be rinsed quickly under cold water before being served. It makes good rice puddings; if you want to disguise the taste of sterilized milk, the addition of honey or cocoa is a good ruse. If you are serving it cold, a couple of tablespoons of Cointreau or brandy does wonders.

SAFFRON (*azafrán*), though far cheaper than in England, still seems exorbitant for such a tiny amount. For anyone who likes their rice yellow at a fraction of the cost, a good substitute is *aditivo colorante*, which is powdered and comes in sachets.

SALAD CREAM—see mayonnaise.

SOUP-MIXES. There is an enormous variety of these, all reasonably priced. Try making one up with fish stock if you have any left over from the previous meal—it is inadvisable to keep it more than a day without a fridge. Tinned soups are far more expensive and very limited.

STOCK CUBES are sold widely.

SALT (*sal*). Cooking salt is cheap and very coarse. If you like a finer grade, ask for *sal de mesa*, mostly sold in polythene bags.

SUGAR (*azúcar*). Cube sugar and brown sugar can be bought everywhere. For granulated, ask for *azúcar molido*. It is mostly prepacked in kilo and half-kilo polythene bags, but in country districts will be ladled out of a sack into brown paper. Don't worry if it looks a bit yellow and less pristine than ours. Icing sugar is usually sold at the *confitería*.

VINEGAR (*vinagre*) is much milder than in England. It can be bought at the grocers in plastic bottles with a little spout which you have to decapitate. If you want to take the remains home, you'll have to transfer it to a bottle with a proper stopper. It can also be bought from the wine shop (*bodega*) straight from the barrel (take your own bottle).

Beverages and Soft Drinks

TEA is available in both packets and tea bags in all the tourist areas and big towns. However, it is very expensive and not particularly good so it is much better to take your own.

COFFEE is served very strong in Spain, so unless you are prepared to heap in endless spoonfuls it doesn't taste too good. It doesn't taste much better if you do make it strong and, although coffee beans aren't dear, it's an extravagant pastime. Instant coffee is a good substitute and on the whole tastes as good as Spanish coffee, but it's expensive—the de-caffeinated sort even more so. The freeze-dried type is now available, also very expensive.

COCOA is reasonably priced and can be bought anywhere. You can also buy 'Nesquik' in chocolate and strawberry flavours which can be mixed with hot or cold milk.

MINERAL WATER. This can be bought anywhere—supermarket, small grocer or wine shop—and comes in bottles for which a deposit is charged, refundable on return. There are both fizzy and still varieties; Insalus and Solares are the least mineral-tasting of the still ones.

FRUIT DRINKS. There is so far only one make of orange squash, which seems strange in a hot, thirst-making climate. It tastes somewhat synthetic, is not cheap and comes in ketchup-size bottles. However, there are several alternatives:

Large bottles of orange, lemon, grapefruit, pineapple, tomato and apple juice. These are good chilled but are quite expensive to drink as a long thirst-quencher and they take up a lot of room in the fridge. The Spanish drink them diluted with mineral water but this makes them very insipid since they are neither concentrated nor very sweet. There are various brands such as Pi-mar and Oransol—both good.

Tinned fruit juices—again delicious chilled, but expensive for long drinks. Flavours like apricot and grape are good made up into jellies.

Fizzy drinks. There are several makes. Fanta produce litre bottles of orange and lemon, which is an economical way of buying and doesn't leave you so cluttered up with empties to take back as the little bottles do. Beware the misleading brand called 'Crush' which sounds like a squash but is just as fizzy as the rest.

Instant mixes. This is a very economical way of making a long drink. One packet mixed with ordinary water will make a litre of either fizzy orange or lemon or still orange, lemon or strawberry. It costs very little but does have a faint tang of Epsom salts.

Non-fizzy sweetened orange and lemon, made by Tri-naranjus, comes in small bottles and is excellent—one of the best drinks we've ever tasted.

If you can take squash out with you, take as much as possible because, there's no doubt about it, it's much the cheapest way of quenching your thirst. However, if anyone in your party is addicted to Coca-Cola or Pepsi-Cola, they are both cheap in Spain. They can be bought in small or litre-sized bottles; the latter cost little more than a small bottle in England.

Bitter lemon, tonic and soda water can all be bought in any tourist area. The soda is generally in small bottles, not syphons (though if you ask for soda in a bar it is called *sifón*!).

Horchata is a special Spanish drink you may like to try. It is sold either in a bar or *horchatería*, and is made from the juice of pressed monkey nuts. It bears a vague resemblance to coconut milk and is said to be very good for you.

You can now buy litre bottles of flavoured milk: strawberry, chocolate and vanilla.

Wines and Spirits

Spanish wine is amazingly cheap and excellent value. For every-day drinking the *corriente* from the barrel costs less than five pence a litre and is much more drinkable than a rough French *vin ordinaire*. A large proportion of it comes from La Mancha, but if you are staying in a wine-producing area, it should be a local wine. If the red tends to be a bit sweet, it is greatly improved by chilling. Some of it has quite a high alcoholic content—up to 18° of alcohol—and if you like to check on this first, ask what the *grado* is, since it is rarely marked on the bottle or barrel.

A visit to the *bodega* (wine shop) is much more interesting than buying wine in a supermarket. Large barrels line the walls, containing not only wine but Spanish-made liqueurs, brandy, vermouth and vinegar. Some *bodegas* are also bars so that you can have a glass of wine before buying it. You take your own bottles to be filled up, or the *bodega* will rent you a *garrafa* (large wicker-covered bottle holding 4 or 16 litres). The deposit is quite hefty, costing more than the wine, but I suppose this is to discourage people from 'whipping' the carafes to make into lamps.

The next price range is table wine, *vino de mesa*, which is marketed under brand names; you pay more for a plastic stopper and a label but it is not nearly as good value as *corriente* from the barrel, and is quite probably the same wine anyway.

The more expensive Spanish wines (which are ludicrously cheap by French standards) are well worth trying. Some are extremely good, particularly those of the Rioja. Wine there is made by the same methods as in Bordeaux, though instead of each grower producing wine from his own grapes there are wine co-operatives which collect the grapes from all the small growers in one area. Chaptalisation (adding sugar) is unknown.

Good or bad years don't assume much importance; the weather is much more consistent than in France, so there is little difference in the quality each year. The ageing of the wine is important and anything less than three years old should be avoided.

The label on the bottle should give the region of origin of the wine (*denominación de origen*)—similar to the French *appellation contrôlée*; we have listed these below, together with the provinces they cover, so that if you happen to be in the area you can try the best local wine.

Denominación de Origen	Provinces
Alella	Barcelona
Alicante	Alicante
Cariñena	Zaragoza, Aragón
Cheste	Valencia
Huelva	Huelva
Jumilla	Murcia
Jerez (sherry)	Cádiz
Málaga	Málaga
Mancha	Albacete, Ciudad Real, Cuenca, Toledo, Mancha
Montilla	Córdoba ⎫ very similar to sherry
Moriles	Córdoba ⎭
Navarra	Navarra
Panadés	Barcelona, Tarragona
Priorata	Tarragona
Requena	Valencia
Ribero	Orense
Rioja	Alava, Burgos, Logroño, Navarra
Tarragona	Tarragona
Utiel	Valencia
Valdeorras	Orense
Valencia	Valencia

Some wine is also produced in Galicia, Castile, the Balearics and the Canaries.

SPARKLING WINE (not allowed to call itself Spanish Champagne) is made by three methods:

1. The *Méthode Champenoise*—the same way as French champagne is made. This is a good drink. Only a wine producer

using this method is entitled by law to call himself *cava,* and *criado en cava* on the label will tell you you're on to a good thing.

2. The *Méthode Cuvée Close* means that the wine is fermented in a tank and then bottled under pressure. This is not harmful but the wine is said to be not as good.

3. Carbonic gas is added to natural still wine. This is the one which has probably given Spanish champagne a bad name. It can be unpleasantly sweet and fizzy and is best avoided.

BRANDY. Spanish brandy is nothing like as good as French but then it is far younger and cheaper. Some of the cheapest stuff can be very nasty—beware the *corriente* from the barrel. The safest bet is to stick to the brands made by the well-known sherry houses like Domecq, Gonzáles Byass or Osborne. French brandy can be bought in most places and costs less than it would in England.

GIN. Some Spanish gin looks startlingly cheap; it also has a slightly sweet, scented flavour. The quality goes up with the price, but the most expensive is still only half the price of gin in England.

WHISKY is available everywhere, and is expensive by Spanish standards.

LIQUEURS. A lot of French liqueurs are sold, some made under licence in Spain, and they are all cheaper than they would be in France. There is a wide range of Spanish liqueurs, including a banana one from the Canaries. Again, the suspiciously cheap ones tend to be low proof and anaemic, particularly those from the barrel. However, they are good value for kitchen use if you are given to pouring Cointreau into fruit salads.

SHERRY. In addition to the labels familiar to us, there are a host of other brands. It makes it less bewildering to find that sherry falls into four categories:

Fino—very dry and pale, excellent served chilled (15° to 16° of alcohol).

Amontillado—dry to medium dry, it is in fact a more aged

Fino (16° to 18°, up to 20° when older).
Oloroso—practically all sweet, rich dessert wines (18° to 20°).
Pedro Ximénez (or P.X.)—extremely sweet, almost treacly (20° to 24°).

You can buy sherry direct from the barrel and if you like a dry one, ask for *corriente fino*, though a request for *vino blanco* often produces dry sherry and not white wine, which is *vino blanco de mesa*. The *bodegas* frequently classify *fino* sherries further, awarding *palmas* for extra quality (rather like stars in brandy); thus *cuatro palmas* is the very best.

The grading for *oloroso* sherry is *cortado*, ranging from one to four *cortados* in the same way.

If you are in the Córdoba area, the Montilla-Moriles wine is very similar to sherry and is perfectly delicious. By the way, anyone who likes a Manzanilla should state clearly that it's sherry (*jerez*) they're after, or they could well end up with some herb tea of the same name.

APERITIFS. The Italian vermouths like Martini and Cinzano are very cheap and are mostly made under licence in Spain. The French ones, Dubonnet for example, cost more but are still good value. A few are sold in miniature bottles but this is more of a gimmick and not economical.

CIDER is made in Spain, chiefly in the Asturias region. Some of it comes in champagne-like bottles and tastes rather like champagne-perry; it makes a light and pleasant drink.

SANGRÍA. This is a refreshing red wine cup which you can buy ready bottled but is easy to make yourself and much cheaper. Recipes vary from one place to the next, but it is basically made with a bottle of red wine, the juice of a lemon and a glass of soda (or a bottle of bitter lemon), two oranges quartered, slightly squeezed and left in, a tablespoonful of sugar and a dash of brandy or Cointreau. Chill for an hour if possible and, just before serving, add ice cubes. Possible variations in the ingredients include sliced peaches and the rind of a cucumber.

BEER is all of the light continental type, whether Spanish, Danish or German.

RECIPES

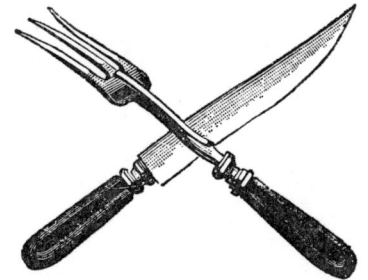

Introduction to Recipes

WEIGHTS AND MEASURES. We have used metric weights where you will need them for shopping. To save a lot of feverish calculations, the easiest way is to forget about converting exactly into ounces and pounds and to think of half a kilo as a pound, and one kilo as two pounds; you'll then get a pleasant surprise because a kilo is in fact worth over 2 lbs. so you always get a bit more for your money.

We give below a conversion table on these lines.

METRIC AMOUNT		APPROX. WEIGHT	FOR APPROX. CONVERSION	SPECIAL NAMES
50 grammes	=	1¾ oz.	2 oz.	
100 gr.	=	3½ oz.	4 oz.	*etto* (Italy)
125 gr.	=	4½ oz.	¼ lb.	
250 gr.	=	9 oz.	½ lb.	*demi-livre* (France)
½ kilo or 500 gr.	=	1 lb. 2 oz.	1 lb.	*livre* (France)
750 gr.	=	1 lb. 11 oz.	1½ lb.	
1 kilo or 1000 gr.	=	2 lb. 4 oz.	2 lbs.	
1 litre	=		1¾ pints	

For other measurements we have used teaspoons, tablespoons, wine glasses and cups. These are all level measures. Spoons have more or less standard sizes but cups vary as much in shape as in capacity. So to help you check the size of cup used in the recipes, we've measured how much it holds in tablespoons and dessertspoons:

1 cup of		*Tablespoons*	*Desertspoons*
Rice	=	9	14
Sugar	=	9	15
Flour	=	10	18
Water	=	11	19

COOKING TIMES. The cooking times given are approximate and naturally depend on the different types of cooker used and whether the gas cylinder is about to run out. We don't imagine that anyone cooking on holiday has never cooked in their lives before, so we have not launched into step-by-step details in the recipes.

Where it is not obvious, the recipes are to serve four people.

Some Cold Dishes

Gazpacho Soup

	FRENCH
¾ litre tomato juice	jus de tomatoes
¼ cup olive oil	huile d'olive
¼ cup lemon juice and a little pulp	citron
1 kilo tomatoes	tomates
1 green pepper	poivron, piment
½ onion	oignon
1 dessertsp. brandy	cognac
salt, pepper	sel, poivre

ITALIAN	SPANISH
succo di pomodoro	jugo de tomates
olio di uliva	aceite de oliva
limone	limón
pomodori	tomates
peperone	pimiento
cipolla	cebolla
cognac	coñac
sale, pepe	sal, pimienta

Peel tomatoes and chop, removing the coarse centre part (or put through a Mouli). Dice the pepper and peeled cucumber and chop the onion finely. In a large bowl mix the olive oil, lemon juice and pulp and tomato juice. Add the chopped vegetables, brandy and seasoning to taste. Add two or three ice cubes and keep in the coldest part of the refrigerator.

Traditionally *Gazpacho* has bread in it, either as breadcrumbs included in the basic tomato juice mixture or as tiny squares of bread served separately. Another variation is to liquidise the pepper and cucumber and add it to the soup, but we prefer the crisp contrast of the chopped vegetables.

Tinned Fish Hors D'oeuvres

	FRENCH
1 large tin tuna fish	thon
1 tin sardines in oil	sardines
1 small tin squid	calmars
(or prawns, shrimps, mussels, etc. as available)	(or crevettes roses, crevettes grises, moules)
3 hard-boiled eggs	oeufs
¼ kilo shelled peas (or equivalent tinned or frozen), cooked and cooled	petits pois
black olives	olives noires
lettuce	laitue

ITALIAN	SPANISH
tonno	atún, bonito
sardine	sardinas
calamari	calamares
(or gamberetti rosa, gamberetti grigi, cozze)	(or gambas, camarones, mejillones)
uova	huevos
piselli	guisantes
olive nere	aceitunas negras
lattuga	lechuga

Drain all fish. In the centre of a serving dish put the flaked tuna, surrounded by the sardines (tails and backbones removed), then a border of squid or shellfish and finally surround with the peas. Slice the hard-boiled eggs and arrange on the peas; sprinkle black olives liberally over the dish. Serve with French dressing or mayonnaise, and the lettuce in a separate bowl.

Tuna Fish Hors D'oeuvre

FRENCH

3 cups flaked tinned tuna	thon
6 tomatoes	tomates
1 large onion	oignon
1 tin anchovies	anchois
½ cup gherkins	cornichons
1 cup olives	olives
dried or fresh mixed herbs	fines herbes
French dressing made with	huile, vinaigre
oil, vinegar, salt, pepper	sel, poivre

ITALIAN   **SPANISH**

tonno	atún, bonito
pomodori	tomates
cipolla	cebolla
acciughe	anchoas
cetriolini marinati	pepinillos
olive	olivas, aceitunas
erbe	hierbas finas
olio, aceto,	aceite, vinagre,
sale, pepe	sal, pimienta

On a serving dish place a layer of tuna, followed by half the tomatoes, sliced. Next comes a layer of raw onion rings, then chopped gherkins, the rest of the sliced tomatoes and finally the olives and anchovies. Sprinkle a pinch of herbs between each layer and cover with a cup of French dressing. This should not be put in the fridge. If you like to use it as a main course, increase the quantities.

Tuna Mayonnaise

	FRENCH
1 lettuce	laitue
1 tin tuna	thon
½ cucumber	concombre
1 apple	pomme
mayonnaise	mayonnaise
capers	câpres

ITALIAN	SPANISH
lattuga	lechuga
tonno	atún, bonito
cetriolo	pepino
mela	manzana
maionese	mayonesa
capperi	alcaparras

Flake the tuna; peel and dice the apple and cucumber, then mix them all with about a cupful of mayonnaise. Serve on a bed of lettuce and decorate with capers.

Tomato and Tuna Jelly

	FRENCH
1 large tin tomato juice	jus de tomates
1 cup flaked tinned tuna	thon
Gelatine or aspic powder—enough for ½ litre liquid	gelatine, gelée en poudre
½ cucumber, peeled and diced	concombre
3 hard-boiled eggs	oeufs
Salt, pepper	sel, poivre

ITALIAN	SPANISH
succo di pomodoro	zumo or jugo de tomate
tonno	atún, bonito
gelatina	gelatina, aspic
cetriolo	pepino
uove	huevos
sale, pepe	sal, pimienta

In a pyrex dish arrange the flaked tuna, diced cucumber and sliced hard-boiled eggs. Dissolve the gelatine in half the tomato juice. Add the rest of the juice, season and pour over the tuna mixture. Leave it to set and serve with salad.

Salade Niçoise

	FRENCH
1 good lettuce (cos or density)	laitue
6 tomatoes	tomates
1 small tin tuna	thon
1 tin anchovies	anchois
4 hard-boiled eggs	oeufs
1 small tin pimento	piments
olives (optional)	olives
oil	huile d'olive
vinegar	vinaigre
salt, pepper	sel, poivre

ITALIAN	SPANISH
lattuga	lechuga
pomodori	tomates
tonno	atún, bonito
acciughe	anchoas
uova	huevos
peperoni	pimientos
ulive	aceitunas
olio d'oliva	aceite
aceto	vinagre
sale, pepe	sal, pimienta

Slice the tomatoes, hard-boiled eggs, and pimento, then put in a salad bowl with the lettuce, olives and tuna, broken up. Decorate with a lattice pattern of anchovy fillets and, before serving, pour over a French dressing made with the oil, vinegar, salt and pepper. A few cold, cooked French beans make a good addition.

Fish (Hot Dishes)

FISH. There are several interchangeable fish that can be used as alternatives to the ones given in the recipes. It's a good plan to go to the market or fishmonger and buy what looks good, find out what it is and then decide how to cook it; this is better than setting out with a preconceived idea of what to buy, finding there isn't any and your mind going a complete blank over what to get instead. Here are a few ideas:

1. LARGER FISH CUT IN STEAKS

	FRENCH
carp	carpe
sturgeon	esturgeon
hake	colin
Fresh tunny	thon frais
swordfish	espadon
salmon	saumon
conger eel	congre
turbot	turbot

ITALIAN	SPANISH
carpione	carpa
storione	esturión
merluzzo, merlano	merluza
tonno, vitello di mare	atún, bonito
pesce spada	pez espada
salmone	salmón
grongo	congrio
rombo maggiore	rodaballo

These are good dipped in egg and breadcrumbs and fried in oil. Equally good poached gently, so they don't fall apart, allowed to get cold and served with mayonnaise, preferably flavoured with lemon. You can also add chopped parsley, capers, gherkins or olives and a few slices of hard-boiled eggs.

2. FISH TO BRAISE ON TOP

	FRENCH
shad	alose
conger eel, eel	congre, anguille
sea bream	dorade, daurade
eel-pout, turbot	lotte
gurnard, gurnet	grondin
sturgeon	esturgeon

ITALIAN	SPANISH
alosa, agoni	alosa, sabalo
grongo, anguilla	congrio, anguila
dorata, orata, dèntice	pargo, dorada
bottatrice	faneca
pesce cappone	gallina del mar, carpón
storione	esturión

These can be done in the pressure cooker, but an enamelled or flameproof earthenware casserole is better for the flavour. We have also used a large frying pan with a lid.

3. FISH FOR GRILLING

	FRENCH
bass, sea bass	bar, loup de mer
weever	vive
perch	perche
trout	truite
flounder	plie
fresh herring	hareng
sole	sole
mackerel	maquereau
red mullet	rouget

ITALIAN	SPANISH
spìgola	lubina, lobo marino
dragone trachino	arana
perca	perca
trota	trucha
passera	platija
aringa	arenque
sogliola	lenguado
lacerto, sgombro	caballa, estornino
triglia	salmonete

Serve with mustard sauce made in a bowl with two teaspoons of Dijon (white wine) mustard to which you add a tablespoon of chopped parsley, 4 tablespoons of barely melted butter. Stir till smooth, then add the juice of half a lemon.

These fish are also good dusted with seasoned flour, then fried in butter and oil (half and half). Serve with extra melted butter, barely brown and foaming straight from the pan.

4. FISH TO BAKE IN THE OVEN

	FRENCH
grey mullet	mulet, muge
red mullet	rouget
sea-bream	dorade, daurade
sea-bass	loup de mer, bar
whiting	merlan
mackerel	maquereau
john dory	saint Pierre, Doré, poule de mer
gurnard, red gurnet	grondin
angler	lotte de mer, baudroie

ITALIAN	SPANISH
muggine, cèfalo	lisa, mújol
triglia	salmonete
dorata, orata	pargo, dorada
branzino, spìgola	lubina
merlano, nasello, merluzzo	pescadilla
sgombro, maccarello	caballa, estornino
sampietro	san Pedro
pesce cappone	gallina del mar, carpón
rana pescatrice, rospo	rape

These are all good baked on a bed of sliced onion, with a glass of white wine poured over. Chopped carrots, leeks, tomatoes and/or pimentos can be included, or a tin of *ratatouille* mixture. You can use melted butter or oil instead of wine and cover with white breadcrumbs.

PREPARATION OF MUSSELS AND CLAMS

Fresh seafoods are often cheap and though the preparation is a bit tedious, the cooking is simple and the flavour so much better than the tinned equivalent that it's worth the effort.

Any mussels or clams which remain open while you are cleaning them, should be smartly discarded.

Wash them thoroughly in several changes of water, removing the 'beards' with a knife and any bits of grit by scrubbing. Put them in a large saucepan, cover and cook over a moderate heat for 5-6 minutes, shaking occasionally. They are ready when the shells have opened (any that refuse should be thrown out). The liquid can be strained and used or, if you need more for a soup, the molluscs can be cooked with white wine—a glass for every litre of mussels. They can be removed from their shells and will keep well in a fridge for a day if not needed immediately.

Provençal Baked Fish

FRENCH

sea bream, bass, rascasse	pagel, daurade, bar, loup de mer, rascasse
½ kilo tomatoes (or 1 large tin)	tomates
½ tin anchovies	anchois
2 cloves garlic	ail
1 glass white wine	vin blanc
1 tablesp. chopped parsley	persil
butter	beurre
salt, pepper	sel, poivre

ITALIAN   SPANISH

pagello, orata spigola, ombrina	lobo marino, dorada, rascacio
pomodori	tomates
acciughe	anchoas
aglio	ajo
vino bianco	vino blanco
prezzemolo	perejil
burro	mantequilla
sale, pepe	sal, pimienta

This should really be baked in the oven, but it can be cooked slowly on top in a casserole or thick saucepan. Ask the fishmonger to scrape off the scales and clean the fish, removing the head. In an oven dish place the peeled, chopped tomatoes, crushed garlic, chopped parsley and pounded anchovy fillets. Sprinkle on a little pepper, then put the fish on top. Pour over the wine, a pinch of salt and dot with butter. Bake in a moderate oven (preheated) for 20 minutes, then carefully turn the fish over, putting some of the tomato mixture on top. Continue baking until the fish is cooked right through.

Baked Herrings Provençale

	FRENCH
(Oven only)	
4 herrings	harengs
½ kilo tomatoes	tomates
2 small onions	oignons
1 tablsp. oil	huile
1 teasp. sugar	sucre
2 tablesps. wine vinegar	vinaigre de vin
1 tablesp. melted butter	beurre
salt, pepper	sel, poivre
parsley to garnish	persil

ITALIAN	SPANISH
aringhe	arenques
pomodori	tomates
cipolle	cebollas
olio	aceite
zucchero	azúcar
aceto di vino	vinagre de vino
burro	mantequilla
sale, pepe	sal, pimienta
prezzemolo	perejil

Butter an oven-proof dish. Skin the tomatoes and cut in quarters. Lightly fry the onions in oil, then put with the tomatoes into the dish. Mix the vinegar, sugar and seasoning together and pour over the tomatoes. Place the herrings on top, brush with melted butter and cover with foil or lid. Bake in a moderate oven for 45 minutes. Sprinkle with chopped parsley and serve.

Catalán Salt Cod

	FRENCH
dried salt cod	morue
3 tablesp. oil	huile
1 onion	oignon
2 tomatoes	tomates
1 green pepper	piment
2 cloves garlic	ail
a sprig of parsley	persil

ITALIAN	SPANISH
baccalà	bacalao
olio di semi	aceite
cipolla	cebolla
pomodori	tomates
peperone	pimiento
aglio	ajo
prezzemolo	perejil

Dried salt cod needs to be soaked a good twenty-four hours in water, which should be changed six times. If it is still too salty, soak for a short while in warm water. It should then be cut into small pieces. Put the oil into a thick saucepan and gently fry the onion until it is golden. Add the chopped tomatoes, crushed garlic, chopped and seeded green pepper and the parsley, followed by the salt cod. Cover with tepid water and cook briskly till the liquid is reduced by half. If you like, add a little sherry or dry vermouth before serving.

Fish with Red Wine Sauce

1 kilo fish	poisson
2 onions	oignons
6 rashers bacon	lard
4 tablesp. butter	beurre
2 tablesp. flour	farine
2 glasses red wine	vin rouge
1 glass fish stock or water	bouillon
125 grms. mushrooms or small tin	champignons
salt, pepper	sel, poivre

pesce	pescado
cipolle	cebollas
pancetta	bacón, tocino
burro	mantequilla
farina	harina
vino rosso	vino tinto
brodo	caldo
funghi	champiñones
sale, pepe	sal, pimienta

Chop the onion and bacon and fry gently in half the butter. Add the rest of the butter, followed by the flour and the wine, poured in gradually and stirred till smooth. Simmer for a few minutes while you cut up the fish. Add the fish pieces and seasoning and either simmer gently on top of the stove or cook in the oven till done—about half an hour. Five minutes before serving, put in the chopped mushrooms. Triangles of bread crisply fried in butter and oil make a good accompaniment.

Fried Fresh Sardines or Anchovies

	FRENCH
fresh sardines or anchovies	sardines or anchois
milk	lait
flour	farine
salt, pepper	sel, poivre
lemons	citrons
olive oil	huile d'olive

ITALIAN	SPANISH
sardine or acciughe	sardinas or anchoas
latte	leche
farina	harina
sale, pepe	sal, pimienta
limoni	limones
olio d'oliva	aceite d'oliva

Unless the fish are very fresh, they should be split open and cleaned. While the oil is heating in a large frying pan or deep fryer, dip the fish first in milk, then in seasoned flour, so that they are lightly coated with it. When the oil is hot enough to brown a cube of bread in a minute, put as many fish in as will float on the surface side by side without getting on top of each other. As soon as they are crisp and golden, remove, keep hot and fry the next batch. Serve immediately with lemon quarters.

Swordfish or Tunny with Lemon and Almonds

FRENCH

1 steak swordfish or tunny per person	espadon (empereur), or thon
butter	beurre
oil	huile
flour	farine
salt, pepper	sel, poivre
lemons	citrons
a few almonds (optional)	amandes

ITALIAN

SPANISH

pesce spada or tonno	pez espada (emperador) or atún
burro	mantequilla
olio di semi	aceite
farina	harina
sale, pepe	sal, pimienta
limoni	limones
mandorle	almendras

Dip the fish steaks in seasoned flour, then fry in butter to which a little oil has been added. When the fish is cooked through and golden brown on the outside (this will depend on the thickness of the slices), put in a serving dish and keep hot. If you are using almonds, add a little more butter and toss the blanched almonds for a few minutes till they are golden brown, then sprinkle them on top of the fish. Squeeze the lemon juice into the pan (allow half a lemon per steak), add a little black pepper, allow to bubble for a minute then pour over the fish.

Basque Rice

	FRENCH
½ kilo rice	riz
½ kilo hake	colin
1 clove garlic	ail
1 onion	oignon
parsley	persil
oil	huile
salt, pepper	sel, poivre

ITALIAN	SPANISH
riso	arroz
nasello	merluza
aglio	ajo
cipolla	cebolla
prezzemolo	perejil
olio di semi	aceite
sale, pepe	sal, pimienta

Chop the onion and fry lightly in the oil. Add slices of hake, chopped garlic and parsley and then the rice. Add boiling water —three times the quantity of the rice. Season and simmer for half an hour or until the rice is cooked, taking care that it doesn't stick to the pan.

Seafood Pancakes with Piquant Sauce

FRENCH

Pancake batter needs:

	FRENCH
flour	farine
½ teasp. salt	sel
1 tablesp. oil	huile
water	

Filling (tinned, frozen or fresh):

	FRENCH
shrimps	crevettes grises
mussels	moules
prawns	crevettes roses (bouquets, langoustines)

Piquant sauce:

	FRENCH
½ litre white sauce	
1 egg	oeuf
1 tablesp. lemon juice	jus de citron

ITALIAN	SPANISH
farina	harina
sale	sal
olio	aceite
gamberetti grigi	camarones
cozze	mejillones
gamberetti	gambas
rosi (scampi)	
uovo	huevo
succo di limone	zumo di limón

Make the pancakes and fill each one with the shellfish mixed together. Keep hot. Make the white sauce with butter, flour, milk and seasoning. Just before serving add the beaten egg and lemon juice, being careful not to let the sauce boil, and pour it over the pancakes.

Chopped cooked chicken and ham also make a good pancake filling, topped with a cheese sauce.

Meat and Poultry

MEAT. Most people prefer to eat meat in restaurants where the quality is more reliable (and if it's not, at least you can send it back!) so bearing in mind this, and the fact that meat in all three countries is expensive, we have not given many recipes in this section. Several of these are for casserole-type dishes using cheaper cuts of meat and requiring gentler cooking to discourage toughness. The ham dishes are not cheap unless you take tinned ham out with you, but they are a useful standby for a quick meal.

Blanquette de Veau

	FRENCH
800 grms. stewing veal	blanquette de veau
2 onions	oignons
1 carrot	carotte
1 glass white wine	vin blanc
1 egg yolk	oeuf
1 tablesp. butter	beurre
1 tablesp. flour	farine
1 dessertsp. lemon juice	citron
All or any of these:	
(1) cloves, (2) parsley, (3) sage, (4) thyme, (5) bay, (6) origano (wild marjoram)	(1) Clous de girofle (2) persil, (3) sauge, (4) thym, (5) laurier, (6) origan

ITALIAN	SPANISH
spezzatino di vitello	ternera para guisar
cipolle	cebollas
carota	zanahoria
vino bianco	vino blanco
uovo	huevo
burro	mantequilla
farina	harina
limone	limón
(1) chiodi di garofano, (2) prezze-molo, (3) salvia, (4) timo, (5) alloro, (6) orìgano	(1) clavos, (2) perejil, (3) salvia, (4) tomillo, (5) laurel, (6) orégano

Dice the carrot and veal. Halve the onions and put a clove in each half. Put them all in a saucepan, cover with water and add the glass of wine and any herbs (in moderation). Bring to the boil, then simmer till the veal is tender (about 1½ hours, pressure-cooking time ½ hour), removing any scum that forms. When the veal is ready, put it into a serving dish, having strained off the stock to keep for the sauce. In a saucepan, melt the butter then add the flour followed by enough stock to make a smooth sauce. (The rather mangled-looking herbs, etc., are not kept.) Just before serving, thicken with the beaten egg yolk and lemon juice (taking care not to bring to the boil), and pour over the veal. Good served with rice or boiled potatoes.

Stuffed Cabbage Leaves

	FRENCH
250 grms. raw mince	boeuf haché
½ cup rice	riz
1 cabbage	choux
2 cups tomato juice	jus de tomates
salt, pepper	sel, poivre

ITALIAN	SPANISH
carne tritata	ternera picada
riso	arroz
cavolo	col
succo di pomodoro	jugo de tomate
sale, pepe	sal, pimienta

Mix the beef and rice. Season with salt, pepper and, if liked, cayenne. Detach the cabbage leaves and blanch for 2 minutes in boiling, salted water (if the stems are very thick, cut them out). Put one heaped tablespoon of the mince mixture on each cabbage leaf, roll them up and put them into a large saucepan or frying pan. Pour over the tomato juice, cover and simmer for 40 minutes. If the juice is all used up, add a little stock or water.

Stuffed Aubergines (Eggplant)

FRENCH

200 grms. mince	boeuf haché
1 aubergine per person	aubergines
1 tin tomatoes (400 grms.)	tomates
1 onion	oignon
2 tablesp. oil	huile
cheese sauce	sauce Mornay
parmesan	parmesan
salt, pepper	sel, poivre

ITALIAN SPANISH

carne tritata	carne picada
melanzane	berenjenas
pomodori	tomates
cipolla	cebolla
olio di semi	aceite
salsa Mornay	salsa Mornay
parmigiano	queso rallado (grated)
sale, pepe	sal, pimienta

Peel the aubergines and blanch them in boiling water for three minutes. Drain, cut in half lengthwise and scoop out some of the flesh. Lay them side by side in a serving dish and keep warm. Meanwhile, sauté the onion in oil, then add the mince and, after a minute or two, the tomato and chopped aubergine flesh. Season and simmer for 10 minutes, then fill the aubergines with this mixture, draining off any excess liquid. Cover with cheese sauce and sprinkle with grated parmesan. If possible, brown in a hot oven or under the grill. This is equally good done with courgettes (baby marrows) which need not be peeled.

Hunter's Lamb

FRENCH

¾ kilo lamb	agneau
1 tablesp. oil	huile
1 tablesp. butter	beurre
1 tin anchovies	anchois
1 tablesp. vinegar	vinaigre
1 glass red wine	vin rouge
1 tablesp. flour	farine
¾ cup hot stock	bouillon
rosemary, sage	romarin, sauge
1 clove garlic	ail
salt, pepper	sel, poivre

ITALIAN | **SPANISH**

agnello	cordero
olio di semi	aceite
burro	mantequilla
acciughe	anchoas
aceto	vinagre
vino rosso	vino tinto
farina	harina
brodo	caldo
rosmarino, salvia	rosmarino, salvia
aglio	ajo
sale, pepe	sal, pimienta

Dice the lamb and brown it all over in the butter and oil in a casserole or large, heavy saucepan. Add the peeled and crushed garlic and as soon as it smells garlicky, sprinkle on the flour. Stir for a minute, then gradually add the stock, wine and vinegar, stirring all the time. Season and add a teaspoon of chopped rosemary and a sprig of sage (or pinch of dried sage). Simmer the lamb till tender (about 40 minutes). Mash the anchovy fillets with a tablespoon of liquid from the casserole, then add to the lamb and simmer for a further 5 minutes. Pressure cooking time is 20 minutes; don't bring to pressure again after adding the anchovy.

Lamb with Peas

FRENCH

¾ kilo lamb	agneau
100 grms. ham	jambon
2 onions	oignons
½ kilo peas (or nearest weight frozen)	petits pois
6 good potatoes	pommes de terre
1 cup stock	bouillon
butter or margarine	beurre/margarine
salt, pepper	sel, poivre

ITALIAN   SPANISH

agnello	cordero
prosciutto	jamón de York
cipolle	cebollas
piselli	guisantes
patate	patatas
brodo	caldo
burro/margarina	mantequilla/margarina
sale, pepe	sal, pimienta

Peel and dice the potatoes (if you want to do this ahead, leave them soaking in salted water). Slice the onions and fry gently in 1-2 tablespoons butter or margarine in a casserole or largish saucepan. Dice the ham and slice the lamb and add them to the onions. Fry slowly till the onions become transparent, then add diced potatoes, shelled peas (if frozen, they don't need to be defrosted first), one cup stock and seasoning. A sprig of rosemary is good, if you can find one. Simmer till the meat is tender and the potatoes cooked—about an hour, or 25 minutes in the pressure cooker from the time of coming to pressure. If it looks a bit dry, add a little more stock.

Pork Chops in Red Wine

	FRENCH
8 small pork chops or cutlets	côtes de porc
2 onions	oignons
4 quartered tomatoes or 1 medium tin	tomates
1 small tin pimentos	piments or poivrons
1 wine-glass red wine	vin rouge
1 cup stock	bouillon
1 dessertsp. brandy	cognac
sugar	sucre
oil	huile
margarine	margarine
salt, pepper	sel, poivre

ITALIAN	SPANISH
costolette di maiale	chuletas de cerdo
cipolle	cebollas
pomodori	tomates
peperoni	pimientos
vino rosso	vino tinto
brodo	sopa
cognac	coñac
zucchero	azúcar
olio	aceite
margarina	margarina
sale, pepe	sal, pimienta

Chop the onions in fairly large pieces and fry in a mixture of oil and margarine. When lightly done, put in a serving dish and keep warm (on top of the pan in which your vegetables are cooking if there is no oven). Sauté the chops in the same pan and when partly cooked add a little wine and seasoning. Finish cooking and transfer to the serving dish, arranging some of the onions on top. Keep warm. Now drain most of the fat from the pan, then pour in the stock, the rest of the wine, tomatoes, chopped pimentos and brandy. Add a dash of sugar and a *bouquet garni* (if available) Simmer till slightly reduced, stirring periodically, then pour over the chops and serve.

Pork Chops with Apple and Brandy

FRENCH

6 pork chops	côtes de porc
4 apples	pommes
butter	beurre
2 tablesp. brandy or calvados	cognac, calvados
salt, pepper	sel, poivre

ITALIAN	SPANISH
costolette di maiale	chuletas de cerdo
mele	manzanas
burro	mantequilla
cognac, grappa	coñac
sale, pepe	sal, pimienta

Peel the apples and cut into rings, then fry gently on each side in butter. Remove and keep hot. Fry the pork chops in butter, 7-10 minutes each side, according to size. When they are cooked, place on top of the apple. Add the brandy to the butter in the frying pan, reduce for a minute or two then pour over the chops. Two tablespoons of cream may be used instead of the brandy.

Jambon Buré (grill or oven only)

FRENCH

For each person:	
1 thick slice cooked ham	tranches épaisses de jambon cuit
1 tablesp. cream	crème
2 tablesp. grated gruyère or emmenthal	gruyère, emmental
pepper	poivre

ITALIAN	SPANISH
fette grosse di prosciutto cotto	lonjas espesas de jamón de York
panna	nata
groviera	gruyère, emmental
pepe	pimienta

Put the slices of ham in a shallow pyrex dish, if possible not overlapping. Cover each slice with cream, then grated cheese. Sprinkle with pepper and place in a hot oven or under a medium grill till the cheese looks brown and bubbling. If you are using the grill, make sure the ham is heated right through.

Ham and Asparagus au Gratin

	FRENCH
4 slices cooked ham	jambon
1 tin asparagus	asperges
4 hard-boiled eggs	oeufs
1 packet cheese sauce mix	sauce Mornay
100 grms. grated gruyère	gruyère

ITALIAN	SPANISH
prosciutto cotto	jamón de York
asparagi	espárragos
uova	huevos
salsa Mornay	salsa Mornay
groviero	gruyère

Drain the asparagus and divide equally between the slices of ham. If the stem looks thick, use only the tips and tender part. Wrap them in the ham and put in a pyrex dish. Cover with a layer of sliced hard-boiled eggs. Make up the cheese sauce mix (or if unobtainable make a cheese sauce with butter, flour, $\frac{1}{2}$ litre milk and grated cheese) and pour over the ham. Sprinkle with grated cheese and brown in a hot oven or under the grill. Alternatively, heat through by putting the dish over the saucepan in which your vegetables are cooking.

Noodles with Ham

FRENCH

½ kilo noodles	nouilles
1 onion	oignon
200 grms. ham	jambon cuit
2 tablesp. butter	beurre
100 grms. gruyère or emmenthal	gruyère

ITALIAN	SPANISH
fettucine, tagliatelle	tallerines
cipolla	cebolla
prosciutto cotto	jamón de York
burro	mantequilla
groviera	emmental

While the noodles are cooking in boiling, salted water, fry the chopped onion very gently in butter till transparent. Add the diced ham. When the noodles are cooked, drain them, then mix them with the ham, onion and grated gruyère. Sprinkle with black pepper and serve.

Rioja Omelette

FRENCH

2 slices ham	jambon de York
200 grms. garlic sausage	saucisse
6 eggs	oeufs
1 small tin pimento (90 grms.)	piments
1 tablesp. oil	huile
salt, pepper	sel, poivre

ITALIAN	SPANISH
prosciutto cotto	jamón de York
salame	chorizo
uova	huevos
peperoni	pimientos
olio de semi	aceite
sale, pepe	sal, pimienta

Dice the ham and sausage (you can use a milder sausage like Frankfurter but it will lack the authentic Spanish flavour). Put them in a large frying pan with the oil. While they are frying, beat the eggs, season them and add the chopped and seeded pimentos. Pour this mixture into the frying pan and stir. When the underneath is cooked, cover the frying pan with a plate moistened with milk. Tip the omelette onto the plate, then slide it back into the pan to cook the other side (if the pan looks quite dry, add a little more oil). When the underneath is golden brown, the omelette is ready to be cut into slices and served.

Croque Monsieur

	FRENCH
beaten egg	oeuf
for each person:	
2 thin slices bread (sandwich loaf)	pain de mie
1 slice ham	jambon
1 slice gruyère or emmenthal	gruyère
mustard	moutarde
oil	huile

ITALIAN	SPANISH
uovo	huevo
pane a cassetta	pan americano
prosciutto cotto	jamón
groviera	emmental
mostarda	mostaza
olio di semi	aceite

Cut the crusts off the bread. Heat the oil in the pan. On half the slices of bread put a slice of ham spread lightly with mustard, followed by a slice of cheese. Top with another slice of bread, then dip the sandwiches on both sides in the beaten egg (which should be seasoned) and fry on each side till golden brown.

Stuffed Peppers

6 green peppers	piments
150 grms. ham or bacon	jambon or lard
3 chopped hard-boiled eggs	oeufs
1 beaten egg	
2 tablesp. white breadcrumbs	pain
1 tablesp. chopped parsley	persil
2 tablesp. butter	beurre
2 cups tinned tomato sauce or tomato purée slightly diluted with stock or water	sauce de tomates, purée de tomates
salt, pepper	sel, poivre

peperoni	pimientos
prosciutto cotto or pancetta	jamón de York or bacón
uova	huevos
pane	pan
prezzemolo	perejil
burro	mantequilla
salsa or concentrato di pomodori	salsa de tomate, pisto manchego
sale, pepe	sal, pimienta

The filling can be made in advance. Chop the onion and ham or bacon and fry in butter. When the onion is transparent, remove from the stove and add the chopped hard-boiled eggs, breadcrumbs, parsley and seasoning. Leave to cool.

Cut the tops off the peppers, remove the seeds from inside and rinse out. Mix the beaten egg thoroughly with the stuffing, then fill the peppers with this mixture. Pack them closely in a saucepan so that they can't fall over, pour on the tomato sauce and simmer till the peppers are tender.

Canadian Savoury

FRENCH

For each person:
1 slice toasting bread — pain de mie
1 large tomato — tomate
2 rashers bacon — lard
2 tablesp. grated cheese
  (Cheddar or gruyère) — gruyère

ITALIAN — SPANISH

pane americano — pan
pomodoro — tomate
prosciutto crudo or pancetta — bacón

groviera — queso rallado

This should be cooked in a hot oven or under a slow grill, but it is possible in a frying pan over gentle heat, taking care that the bread doesn't burn. First toast or crisply fry the bread in hot oil on each side, then put on the bread a layer of sliced tomato, the bacon rashers side by side and sprinkle the grated cheese all over the top. Put in the oven or under the grill till the cheese has all melted and is brown and bubbling on top.

If you can only cook on top of the stove, just fry one side of the bread. Let the pan cool down a bit. Put the tomato, etc., on the fried side, then return the savoury to the pan, adding a little more oil. Cook very gently and by the time the cheese has melted, the bread should be nicely fried.

Milan Rice

	FRENCH
½ kilo rice	riz
½ kilo sausage	saucisse
1 onion	oignon
1 litre stock	bouillon
1 cup grated Parmesan cheese	fromage gratiné (Parmesan)
2 tablesp. oil	huile

ITALIAN	SPANISH
riso	arroz
salsiccia	salchicha or mild chorizo
cipolla	cebolla
brodo	caldo
parmigiano	queso rallada (Parmesan)
olio di semi	aceite

Chop the onion and sausage and fry together in the oil. Add the rice and fry till golden, stirring to prevent it sticking to the saucepan. Add the boiling stock and seasoning. Cook for 10 minutes on a high flame, then add the cheese and simmer for 15 minutes or until the rice is cooked—it should be slightly nutty and not overcooked or it will go soggy.

Chicken Contadini

FRENCH

1 chicken (jointed if possible)	poulet
2 tablesp. cooking oil	huile
1 glass sweet Martini	Martini doux
1 large tin tomatoes (400 grms.)	tomates
1 clove garlic	ail
salt, pepper	sel, poivre

ITALIAN

SPANISH

pollo	pollo
olio di semi	aceite
Martini rosso	Martini dulce
pomodori	tomates
aglio	ajo
sale, pepe	sal, pimienta

Sauté the chicken in the oil in a frying pan. When it is browned on all sides, add the sweet Martini. If you like to risk it, set it alight and when the flames have died down, put the chicken and liquid in a heavy saucepan or casserole (or pressure cooker) with the crushed garlic, tin of tomatoes and seasoning. Simmer for about an hour or until the chicken is tender. Serve with rice or noodles.

Chicken Capilotade

<table>
<tr><td></td><td align="center">FRENCH</td></tr>
<tr><td>1 cooked chicken, cut in pieces</td><td>poulet rôti</td></tr>
<tr><td>2 onions, finely chopped</td><td>oignons</td></tr>
<tr><td>2 tablesp. butter or lard</td><td>beurre, saindoux</td></tr>
<tr><td>1 glass white wine</td><td>vin blanc</td></tr>
<tr><td>1 dessertsp. vinegar</td><td>vinaigre</td></tr>
<tr><td>1 glass stock</td><td>bouillon</td></tr>
<tr><td>1 dessertsp. capers</td><td>câpres</td></tr>
<tr><td>parsley or fresh herbs</td><td>persil, fines herbes</td></tr>
<tr><td>salt, pepper</td><td>sel, poivre</td></tr>
<tr><td>tomato purée</td><td>purée de tomates</td></tr>
</table>

<table>
<tr><td align="center">ITALIAN</td><td align="center">SPANISH</td></tr>
<tr><td>pollo arrosto, allo spiedo</td><td>pollo asado</td></tr>
<tr><td>cipolle</td><td>cebollas</td></tr>
<tr><td>burro</td><td>mantequilla</td></tr>
<tr><td>vino bianco</td><td>vino blanco</td></tr>
<tr><td>aceto</td><td>vinagre</td></tr>
<tr><td>brodo</td><td>caldo</td></tr>
<tr><td>capperi</td><td>alcaparras</td></tr>
<tr><td>prezzemolo, erbe</td><td>perejil, hierbas</td></tr>
<tr><td>sale, pepe</td><td>sal, pimienta</td></tr>
<tr><td>salsa di pomodoro</td><td>salsa de tomate</td></tr>
</table>

Chop the onions and fry gently in butter or lard, till golden. Pour over the wine, vinegar and reduce to three quarters. Add 3 tablespoons of tomato purée, the glass of stock or water, seasoning and chopped parsley or herbs. If you are using a bought cooked chicken, you can make the sauce ahead as far as this stage. Then all you do is re-heat it when you add the chicken pieces and chopped capers. Simmer for a few minutes and if necessary, thicken with some fine white breadcrumbs.

Chicken in Wine and Mushroom Sauce

FRENCH

1 chicken (jointed if possible)	poulet
2 onions	oignons
2 cloves garlic	ail
1 packet mushroom soup mix	crème aux champignons
1 glass white wine	vin blanc
100 grms. mushrooms or 1 small tin	champignons
2 tablesp. butter	beurre
salt, pepper	sel, poivre

ITALIAN **SPANISH**

pollo	pollo
cipolle	cebollas
aglio	ajo
zuppa di funghi	crema de champiñones
vino bianco	vino blanco
funghi	champiñones
burro	mantequilla
sale, pepe	sal, pimienta

Chop the onions and fry gently in 2 tablespoons butter. Add another spoonful of butter, followed by the garlic and chicken. Cook for a few minutes, turning frequently. Sprinkle the packet of soup mix over the chicken, stir it in, then gradually add the wine and a cupful of water. Season and simmer till the chicken is tender (about an hour—pressure-cooking time 35 minutes; both a little less if the chicken is jointed). Slice the mushrooms and add to the casserole 10 minutes before serving. This dish goes well with rice.

A variation on this dish is chicken with asparagus, cooked exactly as above but substituting a packet of asparagus soup mix and tin of asparagus tips for the mushroom soup and mushrooms.

Provençal Kidneys

300 grms. kidney	rognons
3 rashers bacon	lard
1 large tin mixed tomato and pimento (400 grms.)	ratatouille
1 large onion	oignon
2 tablesp. butter	beurre
2 tablesp. brandy	cognac
salt, pepper	sel, poivre

ITALIAN	SPANISH
rognoni	riñones
pancetta	bacón
peperonata	chanfaina or sanfaina
cipolla	cebolla
burro	mantequilla
cognac	coñac
sale, pepe	sal, pimienta

Chop the bacon and onion and fry gently in a little butter in a heavy saucepan, casserole or large frying pan. Add the rest of the butter and the sliced kidneys; sauté on all sides for a minute or two, then pour in the brandy. Add the tin of tomato and pimento mixture, season and simmer for 10 minutes.

If you can't get the mixed tin, separate tins of tomato and pimento will do, but the pimentos will need to be chopped up. Some of the mixed tins include aubergines and courgettes and these are equally delicious.

Liver with Orange

	FRENCH
250 grms. calves' liver	foie de veau
1 onion	oignon
3 oranges	oranges
½ glass red wine	vin rouge
1 tablesp. flour	farine
seasoning	sel, poivre

ITALIAN	SPANISH
fegato di vitello	higado de ternera
cipolla	cebolla
arance	naranjas
vino rosso	vino tinto
farina	harina
sale, pepe	sal, pimienta

Liver gets leathery if cooked too long or kept hanging about, so start your vegetables, rice or whatever you plan to have, well in advance so that their last 10 minutes synchronise with the liver.

While they are cooking, grate the rind of one orange, then squeeze it; peel the other two and slice across, keeping the slices for decoration. Chop the onion and fry for 3 minutes in 2 tablespoons of butter. Cut the liver into thin slices, add to the onion and fry for 2 minutes on each side. Sprinkle with flour, then gradually pour over the wine, orange juice and grated rind; season and simmer for 3 minutes. Serve at once, garnished with orange slices.

Although very good with rice, triangles of fried bread make a less filling substitute. They can be fried in oil before you start on the onion, then kept hot on the serving dish which can cover your vegetable saucepan.

Vegetables, Rice and Eggs

Aubergine and Potato Pie

FRENCH

3 aubergines (eggplants)	aubergines
3 large or 5 medium potatoes	pommes de terre
1 cup stock	bouillon
1 glass white wine	vin blanc
½ cup grated cheese	fromage gratiné
salt, pepper	sel, poivre

ITALIAN	SPANISH
melanzane	berenjenas
patate	patatas
brodo	caldo
vino bianco	vino blanco
parmigiano	queso rallado
sale, pepe	sal, pimienta

Peel and slice the aubergines and soak them in salted water for an hour. Rub the bottom and sides of a saucepan with buttered paper, then in it put alternate layers of aubergine and finely sliced potatoes. Pour on the stock, wine and season. Cover and simmer. After 10 minutes, sprinkle the grated cheese on top, then continue cooking till the potatoes are ready. If you have an oven, you can bake the pie in a casserole, sprinkle grated cheese and breadcrumbs on top, dot with butter and leave uncovered.

Aubergines with Cheese and Tomato (Oven only)

	FRENCH
3 aubergines (eggplants)	aubergines
flour	farine
oil	huile
tin tomato sauce	sauce de tomates
100 grms. parmesan	parmesan
mozzarella	Port Salut or St. Paulin

ITALIAN	SPANISH
melanzane	berenjenas
farina	harina
olio di semi	aceite
salsa di pomodoro	tin pisto manchego or salsa tomate
parmigiano	parmesan
mozzarella	manchego

Peel and slice the aubergines and soak them in salted water for an hour. Drain them, then dip the slices in seasoned flour and sauté slowly in oil till brown on each side. Place half the aubergines in an ovenproof dish, cover with half the tomato sauce, grated parmesan, slices of mozzarella and seasoning. Use up the rest of the ingredients in the same way, then bake in a moderate oven for half an hour.

Braised Courgettes (Squash)

	FRENCH
Courgettes (squash)	courgettes
butter	beurre
salt	sel
pepper	poivre

ITALIAN	SPANISH
zucchini	calabazas
burro	mantequilla
sale	sal
pepe	pimienta

Wash the courgettes then cut into slices, less than $\frac{1}{4}''$ thick. Melt some butter in a frying pan or heavy saucepan. Gently brown the courgettes, then add $\frac{1}{2}$ glass of water and seasoning. Cover and simmer till all the liquid has evaporated. They should not be allowed to get soggy.

The white stalks of chard and chicory can be cooked the same way.

Spinach in Olive Oil

	FRENCH
1 kilo spinach or 2 packets whole leaf frozen spinach	epinards en branches
$\frac{1}{4}$ cup oil	huile
$\frac{1}{2}$ clove garlic	ail
3 chopped hard-boiled eggs	oeufs
thyme (if available)	thym
salt, pepper	sel, poivre

ITALIAN	SPANISH
spinaci	espinaca
olio	aceite
aglio	ajo
uovo	huevos
timo	tomillo
sale, pepe	sal, pimienta

Put washed spinach in a broad-bottomed pan with the oil (preferably olive oil, if you like it). Add seasoning and a pinch of thyme to taste. Keep turning the spinach, adding the finely chopped garlic, and cook over a high flame. When the spinach is soft and dark green, transfer to serving dish and sprinkle the hard-boiled eggs on top.

Spinach Salad

FRENCH

4 cups cold cooked spinach or green beans or cauliflower	épinards, haricots verts, choufleur
olive oil	huile d'olive
vinegar	vinaigre
lemon quarters	citron
salt, pepper	sel, poivre

ITALIAN   **SPANISH**

spinaci, fagiolini, cavolfiore	espinaca, judías verdes, coliflor
olio d'uliva	aceite de oliva
acete	vinagre
limone	limón
sale, pepe	sal, pimienta

Make a french dressing with the oil, vinegar, salt and pepper and pour it over the cold vegetables. It should not be too vinegary because the lemon quarters served with the salad should then be squeezed over it. If you are using green beans, a little chopped parsley wouldn't come amiss.

This is not only a good way of using up vegetables, but you can always cook twice the usual amount for one meal; use one half hot and the second half at the next meal, as a labour-saving accompaniment to cold meat.

Tuscan Beans

FRENCH

2 cups dried haricot beans	haricots blancs
2 cloves garlic	ail
1 tin tomatoes (400 grms.)	tomates
sage (or basil or rosemary)	sauge, basilic, romarin
salt, pepper	sel, poivre
oil	huile

ITALIAN

SPANISH

fagioli	habichuelas
aglio	ajo
pomodori	tomates
salvia, basilico, rosmarino	salvia, albahaca, romero
sale, pepe	sal, pimienta
olio di semi	aceite

Soak the haricot beans in water overnight. Drain them, then put them in a saucepan or pressure cooker with a litre of water, 3 tablespoons of oil, the garlic, tomatoes, seasoning and a sprig of sage, or pinch of dried sage. (If you can't get hold of any, try basil or rosemary instead; this will not give the authentic Tuscan flavour but makes an interesting alternative.) Cover the pan and simmer very gently for about 2 hours or until the beans are tender. (Pressure-cooking time 30 minutes.) The sauce should be reduced to a thick consistency. This dish is equally good hot or cold.

Cauliflower with Mayonnaise

	FRENCH
1 cauliflower	choufleur
3 hard-boiled eggs	oeufs
3 large tomatoes	tomates
mayonnaise or salad cream	mayonnaise
olives	olives
pimento (paprika)	piment

ITALIAN	SPANISH
cavolfiore	coliflor
uova	huevos
pomodori	tomates
maionese	mayonesa
ulive	aceitunas
pimento	pimientón

Cook the cauliflower (but don't overcook it) and let it cool. Arrange the flowerets on a dish with sliced hard-boiled eggs and sliced tomato. Cover with mayonnaise, sprinkle lightly with pimento and garnish with olives.

Mixed Cold Vegetables

	FRENCH
250 grms. green beans	haricots verts
1 small tin peas	petits pois
1 large green pepper	piment, poivron
2 dozen olives	olives
2 hard-boiled eggs	oeufs
2 large tomatoes	tomates
mayonnaise	mayonnaise

ITALIAN	SPANISH
fagiolini	judías verdes
piselli	guisantes
peperone	pimiento
olive	aceitunas
uova	huevos
pomodori	tomates
maionese	mayonesa

The beans and peas should be cooked ahead in separate pans, with butter and a little white wine, then allowed to cool. Wipe the serving dish round with a clove of garlic, then place the vegetables in it in layers: beans, sliced pimento, sliced tomatoes sprinkled with black pepper, peas and finally the sliced hard-boiled eggs laid on top. Scatter over the olives and add a little mayonnaise.

Rice Salad

	FRENCH
4 cups cold cooked rice	riz
4 large tomatoes	tomates
1 cucumber	concombre
a few salad onions	oignons
1 green pepper	piment
2 apples	pommes
2 oranges	oranges
olive oil	huile d'olive
vinegar	vinaigre
salt, pepper	sel, poivre

ITALIAN	SPANISH
riso	arroz
pomodori	tomates
cetriolo	pepino
cipolle	cebollas verdes
peperone	pimiento
mele	manzanas
arance	naranjas
olio d'uliva	aceite de oliva
aceto	vinagre
sale, pepe	sal, pimienta

Peel the cucumber, apples and oranges and cut into squares, rather than slices. Slice the tomatoes and pepper, then add all these, plus the onions, to the rice. Make a French dressing from the oil, vinegar, salt and pepper and pour over the rice mixture.

If you would like to make this a main dish, add two cups chopped cooked ham and some diced salami (optional).

Arroz a la Cubana (Cuban Rice)

For each person:

	FRENCH
1 egg	oeuf
1 banana	banane
½ cup rice	riz
seasoning	sel, poivre
cooking oil	huile

ITALIAN	SPANISH
uovo	huevo
banana	plátano
riso	arroz
sale, pepe	sal, pimiento
olio di semi	aceite

Cook the rice in boiling salted water, drain it and keep hot (if you have no oven, put it in an ovenproof dish over a saucepan of boiling water). Slice the bananas in half lengthwise and fry gently on each side in a little oil. Arrange them on top of the rice. Fry the eggs in oil, put them with the rice and bananas; sprinkle with salt and pepper and serve.

Egg Mousse

FRENCH

6 hard-boiled eggs	oeufs
1 cup mayonnaise	mayonnaise
1 cup white wine	vin blanc
gelatine or aspic powder, for ½ litre	gelatine, gelée en poudre
2 egg whites	
salt, pepper	sel, poivre
olives and	olives
anchovies for decoration	anchois

ITALIAN	SPANISH
uova	huevos
maionese	mayonesa
vino bianco	vino blanco
gelatina	gelatina
sale, pepe	sal, pimienta
olive	aceitunas
acciughe	anchoas

Shell the hard-boiled eggs and mash them up in a bowl with a fork. Add the mayonnaise. Dissolve the gelatine in a little water, add the wine then combine with the egg mixture. Season to taste. Beat the egg whites then fold them in. Pour into a serving dish and when set, decorate with a lattice pattern of anchovy fillets, punctuated by an olive or two.

Sweets

Belgian Bananas

	FRENCH
4 bananas	bananes
2 egg whites	oeufs
1 carton plain yoghourt	yaourt naturel
juice of 1 lemon	citron
2 tablesp. sugar	sucre

ITALIAN	SPANISH
banane	plátanos
uova	huevos
yogurt naturale	yogur natural
limone	limón
zucchero	azúcar

Mash the bananas with a fork, then mix in the sugar, lemon juice and yoghourt. Beat the egg whites till they are stiff, then fold them into the banana mixture. Pour into a serving dish. It can be chilled, but shouldn't sit around for hours because the egg whites may go runny.

Pears in Curaçao

	FRENCH
½ kilo eating pears	poires
1 cup orange juice	jus d'oranges
juice ½ lemon	citron
1 miniature bottle Curaçao	Curaçao
sugar or honey	sucre or miel

ITALIAN	SPANISH
pere	peras
succo d'arancia	jugo de naranja
limone	limón
Curaçao	Curaçao
zucchero or miele	azúcar or miel

Peei the pears and slice them thinly into a serving dish. Pour over the orange and lemon juice and Curaçao. Sprinkle with sugar or stir in a tablespoonful of honey. Chill for at least an hour.

Orange Fritters

	FRENCH
4 oranges	oranges
1 cupful flour	farine
1 egg	oeuf
1 tablesp. brandy	cognac
1 tablesp. olive oil	huile d'olive
salt	sel
sugar	sucre

ITALIAN	SPANISH
arance	naranjas
farina	harina
uovo	huevo
cognac	coñac
olio d'uliva	aceite de oliva
sale	sal
zucchero	azúcar

Make the batter with flour, a pinch of salt, an egg, and gradually beat in the brandy and olive oil. If necessary, add some water; the batter should be of a smooth, coating consistency, not too runny. If you like to make it ahead, it can stand for a couple of hours, but it is not vital.

Peel and slice the oranges, removing any pips. Heat a little oil in a frying pan and when it starts smoking, dip some orange slices in batter and fry them on both sides till they are crisp and golden. Sprinkle the fritters with sugar and serve. Banana or apple fritters are good; the brandy can be omitted for children.

Peaches in Fruit Syrup

	FRENCH
6 peaches	pêches
3 oranges	oranges
1 large lemon	citron
4 tablesp. sugar	sucre

ITALIAN	SPANISH
pesche	melocotones
arance	naranjas
limone	limón
zucchero	azúcar

Put some strips of orange and lemon peel in a saucepan with the juice of the oranges, a little water and the sugar. Heat slowly till the sugar dissolves, then boil for 5 minutes. Peel and slice the peaches (pouring boiling water over them makes the skin come off easily). Add the lemon juice to the syrup, then strain it and pour it over the peaches. Chill before serving.

Broken Biscuit Chocolate Slice

	FRENCH
2 cups crushed biscuits	biscuits
1 tablesp. butter	beurre
1 tablesp. sugar	sucre
1 large bar chocolate (approx. 250 grms.)	chocolat

ITALIAN	SPANISH
biscotti	galletas
burro	mantequilla
azucar	azúcar
cioccolate	chocolate

This is a good way of using up broken, uninteresting or not so fresh biscuits. The best way to crush the biscuits is in a polythene bag or between two layers of paper; just bash them with anything from a rolling pin to a tin of tomatoes. The crumbs shouldn't be too fine; little chunks the size of sultanas.

Melt the chocolate and butter in a bowl over a saucepan of hot water. Add the sugar and biscuit crumbs and mix it to a stiff paste. If it seems too crumbly, add a bit more melted butter to bind it. Put the mixture on to a plate lined with foil or butter paper, press flat with a wooden spoon or another plate, cut into slices and leave to set. Equally good for tea or served with ice-cream. Chopped nuts, glacé cherries or sultanas can also be added.

Bibliography

Cass, Elizabeth. *Spanish Cooking*. André Deutsch, 1968.

Chamberlain, S. and N. *The Flavour of Italy*. Hamish Hamilton, 1967.

David, Elizabeth. *French Provincial Cooking*. Michael Joseph, 1960 and Penguin Books, 1964.

Italian Food. Macdonald, 1954 and Penguin Books (rev. ed.), 1963.

A Book of Mediterranean Food. Rev. ed. Macdonald, 1958 and Penguin Books, 1967

Hughes, Spike and Charmian. *Gateway Guide to Eating in France*. Methuen, 1966

Gateway Guide to Eating in Italy. Methuen, 1968.

Marquis, Vivienne and Haskell, Patricia. *The Cheese Book*. Leslie Frewin, 1966.

Mathiot, Ginette and Nélidow, Sacha. *Je Sais Cuisiner en Vacances*. Editions Albin Michel, Paris, 1959.

Rainbird, George. *Sherry and the Wines of Spain*. Michael Joseph, 1966.

Ray, Cyril. *The Wines of Italy*. McGraw-Hill, 1966.

Reboul, J.-B. *La Cuisinière Provençale*. A. Tacussel, 1895.

Index

Abbreviations: F.= France I.= Italy S.= Spain